THE TRACK
OF THE
IRONMASTERS

A HISTORY OF THE
CLEATOR & WORKINGTON JUNCTION RAILWAY
BY
W. McGOWAN GRADON B.A.

CUMBRIAN
RAILWAYS
ASSOCIATION

CONTENTS

Foreword

Author's Preface

FRONT COVER

Keekle Viaduct about 1917 against a background of Cleator Moor and the fells around Ennerdale with a Furness Railway "Cleator Tank" heading a double mineral train towards Moresby   From a painting by Robert Nixon

Foreword

WHEN McGowan Gradon wrote "The Track of the Ironmasters" over fifty years ago, the line of the Cleator & Workington Junction Railway was more or less as it had been built some 70 years earlier. Only a few sections had been lost, and although the sparse passenger service had disappeared in the early 1930s, the line still fulfilled at least some part of its original purpose – to serve the transport needs of the coal, iron and steel industries of West Cumberland.

Since the 1950s the iron and steel industry in West Cumberland has shrunk to a shadow of its former importance, coal mining has disappeared, and, of the Cleator & Workington Junction Railway, only a few earthworks and bridges remain, known solely to those interested in local industrial history. How many of the bargain hunters at Workington market today realise that the site was once the thriving heart of a locally-based railway company which, at its peak, employed some 300 staff? Over eighty years on from the disappearance of the railway company itself, none of its one-time employees remain with us, and those with memories of its decline get fewer by the year.

The main period of contraction was in the early 1960s, after the closure of Walkmill Colliery at Moresby in November 1961, and of local goods stations on the line, the last of these being Workington Central which closed in May 1964. Traffic also ceased from the High Duty Alloys plant at Distington, leaving only the section between Siddick Junction, Calva Junction and Buckhill for traffic to the former Royal Naval Ammunition Depot (known locally as "The Dump"), and steel works traffic from Moss Bay via Harrington Junction and over the one-time "Lowca Light Railway" to Micklam and Lowca. This survived the closure of Harrington No.10 Colliery in July 1968 as the pit's washery continued to handle coal from Solway Colliery – at Workington – until that in turn closed in May 1973. Closure of the line from Moss Bay to Lowca followed quickly, on 23 May. However, the link from Siddick was to live on precariously for another 21 years until 4 June 1992, with the final closure of the arms depot.

Now much of the line is lost and forgotten. Cuttings have been filled by the tipping of waste, other parts built or ploughed over. The occasional degraded embankment or bridge abutment may raise a query in the minds of a few. At Keekle the viaduct stands as a silent monument to the stirring sights and sounds which once frequented its tracks as heavy mineral trains with three or four engines barked their slow progress up the 1 in 70 grade to Moresby Parks. One section, however, of the Cleator & Workington seems destined to live on as a route – though for walkers and cyclists only – through central Workington and Calva Junction to Siddick, where a new bridge over the A595 has for ever removed the former hazard which necessitated the operation of generations of "low-bridge" buses by Cumberland Motor Services.

When McGowan Gradon was writing "The Track of the Ironmasters" in the early 1950s few sources were available to the railway historian other than local newspapers – and he had close business and family links with the Whitehaven News at the time which was, as he acknowledges, one of his principal sources of information. Since then a myriad of railway history sources have become available which were then closed to McGowan Gradon. Nevertheless McGowan Gradon's books on the railways of Cumbria were fairly pioneering in their coverage of railway companies which were small in the national scene. Despite the passage of some 50 years since he was actively writing his books, neither this one, nor his book on the Furness Railway, have yet been fully supplanted by more recent works. In its re-publication, 125 years after the opening of its main line, "The Track of the Ironmasters" therefore stands as a memorial to local West Cumbrian enterprise and industry of a long past era.

Peter Robinson
Grange-over-Sands

Honorary President, Cumbrian Railways Association
July 2004

Note to readers

The text of the original publication has been reproduced precisely in this new edition with the exception of a few obvious typographical errors. However, a series of notes has been inserted after each chapter to correct, update or amplify statements in the original, and these have been supplemented by some new appendices to enhance the value and interest of the book to modern readers.

The Cumbrian Railways Association always welcomes the opportunity to add new photographs to it's collections. If you have, or know of, any photographs which could possibly be of interest to us, please contact the photographic services officer at Bay View, Cat Tree Road, Grange-over-Sands, Cumbria LA11 7EB.

The Cumbrian Railways Association is the local railway history group for Cumbria and North Lancashire. With a membership of around 350 it is a registered charity with the aim of promoting interest in and knowledge of the railways of this area, and the part they played in its development over the last 150 years.

Station master and staff at Distington.   *CRA Pattinson Collection PA0609*

The text of the original edition of *Track of the Ironmasters* by W. McGowan Gradon (Altrincham 1952.) is used here by arrangement with the copyright holder, Michael Moon. In giving his permission, it is Michael's wish that it will be used in order to produce a version of this popular book for a new generation of readers in the 21st century.

Additional notes & text © Peter Robinson 2004
Maps © Peter Robinson/Alan Johnstone 2004
Gradient diagrams © Michael Peascod 2004
Photographs as credited

**Published by the Cumbrian Railways Association,
104 Durley Avenue, Pinner, Middlesex HA5 1JH**

**The Cumbrian Railways Association is registered charity No. 1025436
www.cumbrian-rail.org**

Membership Secretary, 36 Clevelands Avenue, Barrow-in-Furness, Cumbria LA12 0AE

Design and layout by Michael Peascod

Printed by Lambert Print & Design, Settle, North Yorkshire

ISBN 0-9540232-2-6

Author's Preface

This is the story of Cumberland's "junior" railway: the last of all the "little" lines which sprang into being during the rapid development of the iron and coal trade in the county during the early and middle part of the 19th century.

The Cleator and Workington Junction Railway was a veritable David amongst a host of Goliaths. The sturdy individualism of a group of industrialists who fought against the domination of the bigger railways brought the railway into operation.

Iron and steel; coal and coke: these were the commodities which constituted the life-blood of the Cleator and Workington Junction Railway. During the 45 years of its independent existence the "Track of the Ironmasters" never "hit the headlines," or earned phenomenal dividends like its bigger and richer neighbours.

Nevertheless, the Company played a big part in the development of transport facilities for the complex of iron and coal mines; blast furnaces and quarries sited within the territory it served.

As with other railway histories I have undertaken, I am grateful to the Public Relations Department of what is now ponderously styled the London Midland Region of British Railways for information supplied and to The Whitehaven News Ltd. for placing their newspaper files at my disposal. I am also grateful for much encouragement and assistance from other quarters in the compilation of this little book.

W. McGowan Gradon,

Altrincham, 1952.

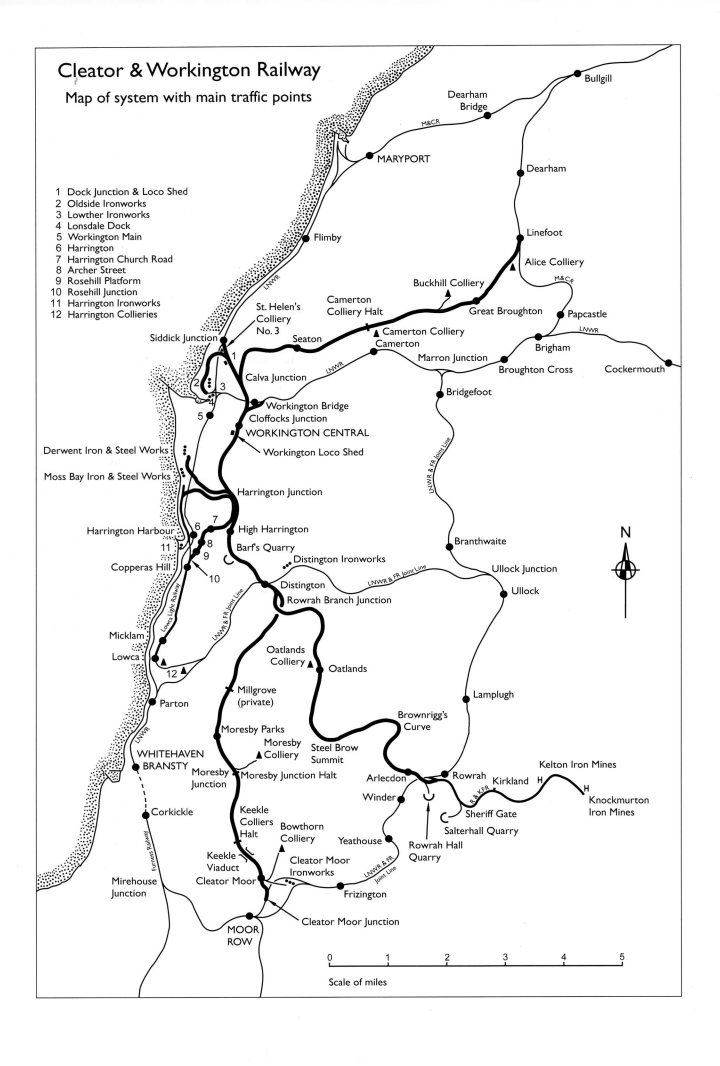

Cleator & Workington Railway

Map of system with main traffic points

1 Dock Junction & Loco Shed
2 Oldside Ironworks
3 Lowther Ironworks
4 Lonsdale Dock
5 Workington Main
6 Harrington
7 Harrington Church Road
8 Archer Street
9 Rosehill Platform
10 Rosehill Junction
11 Harrington Ironworks
12 Harrington Collieries

Bullgill

Dearham Bridge

MARYPORT

M&CR

Dearham

Linefoot

Alice Colliery

Buckhill Colliery

Great Broughton

M&CR

Papcastle

Flimby

Camerton Colliery Halt

Camerton Colliery
Camerton

Marron Junction

Brigham

LNWR

Broughton Cross

Cockermouth

St. Helen's Colliery No. 3

Siddick Junction

Seaton

1

Calva Junction

LNWR

Bridgefoot

2
3

4

Workington Bridge
Cloffocks Junction

5

WORKINGTON CENTRAL

Workington Loco Shed

Derwent Iron & Steel Works

Moss Bay Iron & Steel Works

Harrington Junction

LNWR & FR Joint Line

7

High Harrington

Branthwaite

Harrington Harbour

6

8

Barf's Quarry

Distington Ironworks

Ullock Junction

11

9

Copperas Hill

10

Distington

LNWR & FR Joint Line

Ullock

Lowca Light Railway

Rowrah Branch Junction

LNWR & FR Joint Line

Micklam

Lowca

Oatlands Colliery

Oatlands

12

Lamplugh

Parton

Millgrove (private)

Brownrigg's Curve

Moresby Parks
Moresby Colliery

Steel Brow Summit

WHITEHAVEN BRANSTY

LNWR

Arlecdon

Rowrah

Kelton Iron Mines

Kirkland

H

Moresby Junction

Moresby Junction Halt

Winder

R & KFR

Sheriff Gate

Knockmurton Iron Mines

H

Corkickle

Keekle Colliers Halt

Bowthorn Colliery

Yeathouse

Rowrah Hall Quarry

Salterhall Quarry

Furness Railway

Keekle Viaduct

Cleator Moor Ironworks

Cleator Moor

LNWR & FR Joint Line

Mirehouse Junction

Cleator Moor Junction

Frizington

MOOR ROW

N

CHAPTER I

THE FIRST TEN YEARS

TO appreciate the circumstances which brought the Cleator and Workington Junction Railway into being, a brief survey of the railway facilities as they existed in the industrial west of the county of Cumberland in the 1870s may help the reader. Linking Whitehaven and Workington with the north and east were the Maryport and Carlisle and the London and North Western Railways. The latter was in the peculiar circumstances of only owning the former Whitehaven Junction and Workington and Cockermouth Railways; but Euston kept in touch with this isolated portion of its domain by means of working the Cockermouth, Keswick and Penrith Railway, and also having running powers over the metals of the Maryport and Carlisle Company. [1]

Down to 1879, the rich iron ore bearing country lying east and south of Whitehaven was served by the Whitehaven, Cleator and Egremont Railway, while Whitehaven itself was the northern terminus of the Furness Company.

Between them, these various railways busied themselves in handling the vast output of iron ore, coal, limestone, and pig iron produced from the multitude of mines, quarries, and blast furnaces which not only littered the face of West Cumberland, but stretched in an almost unbroken line from north of Maryport to Carnforth on the shores of Morecambe Bay.

Like the man in the Bible who "waxed fat and kicked," the two companies, which had a stranglehold on the rail traffic between Maryport and Egremont (the L. and N. W. R. and the W. C. and E. R), were anxious to maintain the double-figure dividends with which they had been regaling their shareholders in the 60s and 70s. Furthermore, Euston, in 1878, by acquiring the W. C. and E. R. (modified a year later by joint ownership with the Furness Railway) had tightened its grip on the large and lucrative mineral traffic in the area.

Cumbrians have always been noted for their independence, and when the W. C. and E. increased their freight charges in 1873 (an action promptly copied by the North Western and Furness Companies), the ire of local ironmasters was thoroughly aroused. In 1874 they propounded a scheme for an independent railway from Cleator Moor to Workington and on to Maryport. Their scheme found ready support from the local landowners, Lords Lonsdale and Leconfield, and Mr H. F. Curwen of Workington. [2] A Bill was soon presented to Parliament and came before the Select Committee in March, 1876. At a Protest Meeting over the increased North-Western rates, held in October, 1875, at Workington, it had been revealed that the proposed line should run from Cleator Moor via Keekle and Weddicar to Workington and thence to Siddick and Maryport.

Public opinion about the treatment of traffic and the high rates charged was summarised in one of the local newspapers, which made a violent attack on the L. and N.W.R. and other companies for the high rates, poor services, and dirty and inadequate rolling stock provided for West Cumberland.

The C. and W. J. R. Bill, was, of course, most strenuously opposed by both the North-Western and Whitehaven and Egremont Companies, but after a lengthy hearing, it was approved. Sir Edmund Birkett, Q.C., appeared for the promoters of the new line, one of whose principal champions was Mr. W. Fletcher, F.G.S., J.P., of Cockermouth. In the course of his evidence before the Committee, Mr. Fletcher said the presence of coal measures along the course of the proposed line (at Moresby) was even more important than the iron traffic which would certainly accrue. He also made the remarkable allegation (afterwards withdrawn as erroneous) that the Midland Railway had got "secret" running powers into West Cumberland. [3]

The C. and W. J. R. was incorporated in June, 1876, and soon afterwards the construction of the line, which was entrusted to Messrs. Ward, was started. The initial estimate for the 15 miles of track, for which powers to construct were obtained, was £150,000. Soon it became clear that the line was going to cost a good deal more, and, at the same time, the Furness Railway, the Directors of which evidently realised that the new concern meant business, came forward and offered their support. This took the form, in June, 1877, of the F. R. being empowered to work the "Track of the Ironmasters." [4]

It was also agreed that if the C. and W. J. should ever decide to transfer their railway to any other concern the Furness should have the option over all other interested parties. In 1878 the Furness were empowered to buy shares in the C. and W. J. R.

While the construction of the "main line" from Cleator Moor to Workington was getting under way, a branch from Distington to Rowrah, 6¹/₂ miles, was authorised in July, 1878, together with a short line into Distington Ironworks.

The branch to Rowrah was constructed to link up at the latter place with the Rowrah and Kelton Fell (Mineral) Railway. This railway, another link in the "chain" of ironmasters' interests in West Cumberland, had taken a poor view of the through facilities and high rates charged by the L. and N. W. and Furness Joint Railway, which, up to the construction of the Distington-Rowrah branch of the C. and W. J., provided the only link for the R. and K. F. (M.) R. with the "outer world." [5]

The history of the Rowrah and Kelton Fell line is dealt with later in this book.

The opening of the C. and W. J. main line from Cleator Moor to Workington in October, 1879, was celebrated by a dinner at the Assembly Rooms in Workington on October 18th. The chairman of the Company, Mr. H. F. Curwen, in his speech, dealt at some length with the agreement made with the Furness Railway, which, he felt, would be a good thing for both railways. He also referred somewhat humorously, albeit with a touch of sarcasm, to the small and ancient passenger coaches provided by the F. R. for trains on the C. and W. J. line.

The first directors of the railway were Messrs. Fletcher, R. Alleyne Robinson, J. R. Bain, J. S. Ainsworth and R. Jefferson. All these gentlemen had interests in either local iron ore mines or blast furnace plants. Mr. J. R. Bain was chairman of the Harrington Ironworks, and Mr. Robinson was on the Board of Messrs. William Baird, the Scottish firm of ironmasters who promoted the Rowrah and Kelton Fell (Mineral) Railway.

In 1880 a dividend of 3 per cent. was declared and the following year an additional half per cent. was added. Traffic receipts were about £550 per week.

It had been originally intended to extend the railway northwards from Workington to Maryport, but, in 1881, this extension was dropped. Instead a new Bill for an extension to Brayton Junction, on the Maryport & Carlisle Railway, north of Maryport, was put forward in 1882. The idea was to link up with the Solway Junction Railway at that point. Over this move a quarrel broke out with the M. and C. Company, who foresaw the C. and W. J. collaring the bulk of the iron traffic from West Cumberland to Scotland, which was considerable in those days. [6]

Here is a typical traffic return for one week in July, 1882. Passengers, 1,251 (£27); general merchandise, 1,005 tons (£40); minerals, 13,009 tons (£549); total for week, £616. A dividend of 4¹/₂ per cent. was paid in 1882, and the same year marked the opening of the blast furnaces of Messrs. Charles Cammell at Workington. [7]

Powers were obtained in 1883 to extend to Brayton Junction and an additional sum of £13,400 was borrowed for the purpose. The previous year £42,000 had been raised by creating 4,200 shares of £10 each, bearing interest at the rate of 4¹/₂ per cent.

In 1883 there loomed up one of those periodic slumps that hit the iron trade from time to time. This brought a drop of 60,000 tons in the amount of minerals and freight carried. The slump lasted for the next couple of years.

In spite of this the Company pressed on with its plans for further development. By the spring of 1885 construction of the Moss Bay branch, and a connecting spur from Cloffocks Junction (Workington) to Workington Bridge on the L. and N. W. R. Workington-Cockermouth line were completed. Meanwhile, in spite of the general falling off in traffic, the Rowrah branch freight loading rose to 100,000 tons annually. A 4 per cent. dividend was again paid in 1885.

But the pit of the slump was reached in 1886, when the new chairman, Mr. W. Fletcher, of Brigham Hill, said in his opening remarks at the March half-yearly meeting: "I assure you, gentlemen, it is not a pleasant position for the Board of Directors to have to meet their shareholders entirely empty-handed."

Having got over this gloomy opening, Mr. Fletcher went on to say that the long-hoped-for revival in the iron trade had set in. Four additional blast furnaces had been lit in the area and traffic receipts, which had been down by £3,000, were up by £1,000 in the first seven weeks on the period just begun.

Speaking about the branch to Moss Bay, Mr. Fletcher said that although it had been built specially to tap traffic from the works of the Moss Bay Iron Company the latter had no interest in its construction. In fact they (the C. and W. J. R.) were not offering any traffic facilities which Moss Bay did not already get from the North-Western Railway. Nevertheless, before the branch was made an assurance was obtained from the Moss Bay Company that the share of the traffic given to the Cleator and Workington line would give them "an ample return upon the cost of the branch." Could it be more than a co-incidence that Mr. J. Valentine, a director of the Moss Bay Iron Company, now had a seat on the Board of the C. and W. J. R. ?

Also announced by the Chairman at the March, 1886, meeting, was the settlement of the quarrel with the Maryport and Carlisle Company over the proposed C. and W. J. extension to Brayton Junction. It had been mutually agreed that the "Northern Extension" line should now join the Maryport and Carlisle's Derwent Branch (from Bullgill to Brigham) at Linefoot. Here a junction and exchange sidings were to be put in. At the conclusion of his remarks about the new plans for the Northern Extension line Mr. Fletcher indulged in a crack at "the old enemy" – the North-Western – in these words:

"When it (the extension) has been accomplished and we have, by means of the line to Linefoot, broken through the cordon by which we are hemmed in and shut off practically altogether from the outside world by the London and North-Western Railway I have the utmost confidence that we shall see the end of our troubles." These remarks were greeted with loud applause from the meeting. Although by August of the same year only 23 out of the 40 blast furnaces served by the C. and W. J. were blowing, the slight improvement in trade enabled a 1½ per cent. dividend to be declared.

The agreement with the M. and C. R. had now been signed and work on the extension to Linefoot was put in hand. The borrowing of £17,000 under the C. and W. J. Act of 1885, and bearing a 4 per cent. rate of interest, was applied to the cost of the new works.

Brisker trade enabled Mr. Fletcher to tell a much more cheerful story in March 1887. For the first time the weekly traffic revenue reached four figures. The Moss Bay branch was now making a goodly contribution to the volume of traffic and the opening of the Workington Bridge spur was bringing East Coast coke off the Cockermouth line for Distington and Cleator Moor furnaces over the C. and W. J. instead of being routed via Marron Junction, or round via Whitehaven. In April, 1887, the Northern Extension line was completed from Calva Junction to Linefoot and opened for traffic. [8] Steel sleepers were used on this section, the Chairman commenting on their successful use at the 1888 meeting, when revenue was up by £200 a week and a dividend of 3¼ per cent. declared. Mr. Fletcher was also able to tell shareholders that their railway, now 29 miles long, was virtually completed and had cost, in all, £580,000, almost exactly £2,000 per mile.

Notes to Chapter One

1.   The London & North Western Railway had no general running powers over either the Maryport & Carlisle Railway or the Cockermouth, Keswick & Penrith Railway, though it was empowered by statutory agreement to work all the passenger and goods services on the latter line, the North Eastern Railway having a similar agreement to work mineral traffic over the CK&PR. In the later years before grouping in 1923, the LNWR and M&CR interworked passenger trains between Carlisle and Whitehaven, removing the need to change engines at Maryport. The LNWR did have running powers over two very short sections of the Maryport and Carlisle Railway, these being from Maryport Junction into Maryport station, and over a short section of the Derwent Branch from Brigham Junction to Papcastle, for access to the limestone quarries there. To access its Whitehaven Junction and Cockermouth & Workington lines in West Cumberland the LNWR would have to pay either of the Maryport or Keswick companies, as appropriate.

2.   Landowners who less than ten years earlier had quite happily sold out their interests in the Whitehaven Junction and Whitehaven & Furness Junction Railways to the London & North Western and Furness Railways respectively. For details of the directors of the company see Appendix E.

3.   Not only did the Whitehaven, Cleator & Egremont Railway Company mount a very strong opposition to the proposed new railway, it also proposed two competing lines of its own, extending from its branch, authorised in 1875 from Ullock to Gilgarran colliery, onwards via Distington to Parton, for Whitehaven, and to Workington with connections into the main iron works. In an Act of 1876, powers were granted for the former, but the latter failed as it would have run largely alongside the LNWR. The Whitehaven Branch was not completed until 23 October 1879 for goods traffic, after the WC&ER had succumbed to approaches for a take-over by the LNWR, which became effective from 1 July 1877, later amended to joint ownership with the Furness Railway from the following year (see also note 4 below).

The Queen's Counsel who represented the C&WJR was Sir Edmund Beckett, not Birkett.

The Cleator & Workington Junction Railway Act 1876 authorised:

> Railway No 1: from a junction with the Whitehaven, Cleator & Egremont Railway at Cleator Moor Junction to a junction with Lord Lonsdale's railway at Workington Dock (11.5 miles).
>
> Railway No 2: from Railway No. 1 at Dock Junction to a junction with the LNWR Whitehaven Junction line at Siddick (0.25 miles).
>
> Railway No 3: from Railway No. 1 at Harrington Junction to Rosehill Junction (1.3 miles). Here it would connect with James Bain & Co.'s private mineral line from Lowca to Harrington Harbour, part of which was later to become the Harrington and Lowca Light Railway (see chapter 5).
>
> Railway No 4: from Railway No. 1 at Harrington Junction to near New Yard, Workington, to become known as the Derwent Branch, serving the works of the Derwent Hematite Iron & Steel Co. (1.4 miles).

4.   The C&WJR Bill of 1877 was originally intended to seek powers to extend the railway northwards from near Calva, to a junction with the Maryport & Carlisle Railway near Dearham. From there the C&WJR sought running powers over the M&CR to the junction with the Solway Junction Railway at Brayton. Southwards, the C&WJR also sought to build an extension to near Egremont. These proposals were withdrawn in the face of strong opposition from the LNWR and M&CR, and on the advice of Sir James Ramsden, General Manager of the Furness Railway, when the LNWR agreed that its takeover of the WC&ER be modified to joint ownership with the FR, and the signing of a working agreement between the C&WJR and the Furness Railway on 6 April 1877. The Bill was then amended and enacted, principally to endorse this working agreement, and a traffic agreement on the division of ore traffic from the Cleator and Egremont areas to Workington between the C&WJR, the WC&ER and LNWR.

The terms of the Working Agreement were that the Furness Railway would work all traffic on the C&WJR main line from Cleator Moor to Siddick and Lonsdale Dock. For passenger, goods, pig iron and spiegel (a compound of iron, carbon and manganese) traffic the Furness Company would receive one third of gross receipts, and on mineral traffic 35%, the Furness Railway providing all necessary motive power and rolling stock. A supplementary agreement applied the same terms to the Northern Extension while the C&WJR worked the other branches with its own locomotives.

5.   Gradon seems to have been confused here. At the time of the promotion of the C&WJR Rowrah Branch, the LNWR had not yet moved to take over the Whitehaven, Cleator & Egremont Railway. The R&KFR first contacted the promoters of the C&WJR as early as November 1875 when the Rowrah company was encountering serious problems reaching agreement with the WC&ER over junction arrangements at Rowrah, though agreement was eventually reached to enable to the R&KFR to open. However, it was not until August 1877 that the C&WJR Board agreed to meet directors of the R&KFR to discuss the promotion of a Bill in the 1877/78 Parliamentary Session to build the Rowrah Branch.

6.   The ambitions of the C&WJR to extend both north and south to bypass the lines of both the LNWR and the WC&ER were far from spent. The 1880 plans were for a proposed extension from just south of Siddick, running about half a mile inland from the LNWR, to Maryport, making a junction just north of the station, and with a branch to the docks and the Maryport and Solway iron works on the south side of the town.

In 1881 proposals were once again put forward for a Northern Extension, this time a steeply graded 17 mile line extending right through to a junction with the Solway Junction Railway at Brayton. The following year saw a revised scheme with an east, rather than west, facing junction at Brayton, and powers were granted by an Act of 1883, again in the face of strong opposition from the LNWR and M&CR.

The 1883 Act also included powers for a branch leaving the Derwent Branch near Salterbeck, to cross over the LNWR Whitehaven Junction line at Moss Bay, where a connection

Keekle Viaduct under construction c. 1878.

would be made into the ironworks. It would then run along the shore to Harrington Harbour, with separate branches to serve quays to the north and south, the latter also connecting with the lower end of Bain's tramway from Lowca, with a connection into Harrington Ironworks. These lines were constructed to become the Moss Bay (opened 1885) and Harrington Harbour Branches. Two further short lines at Harrington were also proposed: the first would have run from Rosehill Junction round the northern slopes of Copperas Hill, overlooking the ironworks, and from this a short spur would provide a high level connection over the LNWR, direct into the ironworks. A line was also proposed into Distington Ironworks, designed to make a south facing junction to facilitate traffic from Moor Row.

7.   Charles Cammell & Co. Ltd., took over the works of the former Derwent Hematite Iron Co. which had been established in 1873. Cammells had operated from 1837 at several works in the Sheffield area, and, in about 1870, built a steel works and rail mill at Dronfield in North Derbyshire.

Considering its business to be seriously disadvantaged by its location remote from both ports and sources of iron ore, in 1882 the Company purchased the Derwent Works at Workington, and moved its plant, production and workforce there from Dronfield in the following year.

8.   The West Cumberland iron and steel industry at this time was heavily dependent on supplies of coke from the Durham and Northumberland coalfields. The Northern Extension allowed a large proportion of this traffic from Northumberland, coming from Carlisle via the Maryport & Carlisle Railway, to be routed away from the coastal line and to run via Linefoot and Calva to Harrington Junction, from where it was distributed to customers down the Moss Bay and Derwent branches. Similarly, coke supplies from South Durham, coming via the North Eastern Railway over Stainmore and the Cockermouth, Keswick and Penrith Railway, reached the C&WJR via the curve which linked from the Cockermouth & Workington line at Workington Bridge to Cloffocks Junction, thence again to Harrington Junction.

The Start
Cleator Moor Junction viewed in the early years of the 20th century. While a LNWR 2-4-2 tank heads north with a passenger train for Workington via Marron Junction, FR 0-6-0 No. 119 shunts a line of chaldron wagons in the exchange sidings. Another tank locomotive stands bunker towards the camera on the intervening track. On the left is the Montreal No. 4 Iron Ore Mine, one of the most productive in the Cleator Moor area. CRA Pattinson Collection PA0581

The Destination
Oldside Ironworks at Northside, Workington. Supplies of iron ore, coke and limestone for the iron and steel industry were the principal traffic on the railway. CRA Collection M00191

CHAPTER II

1887 - 1923

TO anyone who has read reports of the Annual General Meetings of railway and other companies, it will be a familiar fact that nearly every concern possessed at least one shareholder who was a regular and severe critic of the Directors and their policies at almost every meeting. The Cleator and Workington Junction was no exception in this respect. A certain Mr. Kitchen was the arch-critic, who raised his voice so regularly at meeting after meeting. Usually, like his counterparts in other companies, any item of expenditure in the least out of ordinary, was Mr. Kitchen's main target. Just as Mr. Marks, of Cockermouth, criticised the proportion of the cost of Penrith Station, which had to be borne by the Cockermouth, Keswick and Penrith Railway, so Mr. Kitchen complained of the C. and W. J. R.'s share of the cost of Distington station. The latter was jointly owned with the London and North Western and Furness Companies by reason of their Gilgarran branch, from Ullock Junction to Parton Junction, passing through Distington.

Another of Mr. Kitchen's complaints concerned the freight rates, which he thought were too low. He seems to have got the idea that, since most of the Directors of the railway were also local ironmasters as well, they were probably keeping the rates down to save themselves money, thus reducing profits for the line. Thus Mr. Kitchen and his fellow shareholders would get lower dividends. In spite of his criticisms, however, the Directors seem to have had a certain liking for their critic, for, some years later, when illness prevented his attendance, a resolution wishing him a speedy recovery was moved by the author's grandfather and warmly supported by the Board.

From 1887 (the year during which the "Track of the Ironmasters" was completed in full) the Company made steady progress. Naturally, the periodic slumps which hit the West Cumberland iron trade from time to time hit the little C. and W. J. pretty hard, and the coal strike in the spring of 1892 was a heavy blow. For nearly four weeks the local furnaces were idle. In his speech at the half-yearly meeting in August, 1892, the Chairman (Mr. William Fletcher) said "As we have been more than any of our neighbours depending on the mineral traffic, which was particularly affected by the strike, I need hardly say that we suffered even more than our neighbours . . . In consequence . . . for the first time in our history, we are unable to pay the preferential dividend in full."

However, two years later, the situation had improved, and, after all the preference dividends had been met in full, the ordinary shareholder got $1^1/2$ per cent. In the meantime, the managing director of Messrs. Charles Cammell and Co., Mr. Wilson, of Sheffield, had joined the C. and W. J. Board of Directors. [1]

Progress from 1900 onwards was steady, rising to the peak year, 1909, when the mineral tonnage carried exceeded 1,600,000 tons. In the meantime, more attention was being paid to the passenger side of the railway. More workmen's trains were put on, and, in the summer, certain through excursions were put on, including one to Silloth via the Northern Extension, the M. and C. Derwent Branch, and the Solway Junction line from Brayton Junction to Abbey Junction. These were, of course, worked by Furness engines and stock.

Just 12 months before the outbreak of the 1914-18 War the "Track of the Ironmasters" was in a healthier condition than ever before.

Although the coal strike of 1911 cut the traffic receipts down by £3,500, expenditure was also down by £3,000 and a $3^1/2$ per cent. dividend was paid. The opening of a battery of coke ovens at Whitehaven reduced the East Coast coke traffic over the line. At the Annual General Meeting in February, 1912, our old friend, Mr. Kitchen, expressed his pleasure that expenditure was so much reduced. The following year mineral traffic fell by £9,000, but under other headings, receipts were £1,000 up. Traffic expenses fell again by £3,000. A 3 per cent. dividend was declared, and Mr. J. S. Randles was congratulated by the Chairman on his knighthood. [1]

Cheers greeted the Chairman's announcement, at the end of the 1913 meeting, that the standard the C. and W. J. set for permanent way was that of the London and North Western Railway. A profitable traffic in manganese ore from Barrow to Workington (which the "Track of the Ironmasters" handled via Sellafield) had developed. Efforts were also being made to get the shares of the Company quoted on the London Stock Exchange. A 5 per cent. dividend was declared.

An even brighter picture was presented for the past 12 months when the shareholders assembled at Workington in February, 1914.

The whole of the main lines had been relayed, with the exception of about three miles. The cost of this had been met out of revenue. Over £4,800 had been spent in 1913 on that account.

The number of passengers carried was up by 500,000 fares, and earnings under this heading increased by £1,275. Mineral traffic exceeded $1^1/_2$ million tons. By now all the chaldron wagons had been withdrawn and replaced by modern vehicles. Other developments included the erection of a "halt" platform at Rosehill (Harrington) on the Lowca Branch; alterations to Arlecdon station; putting in a new siding at Cleator Moor, and the spending of a considerable sum on a new coal conveyor at Lonsdale Dock, Workington.

Other plans, which the war unhappily cancelled, included the provision of further "halt" platforms at Westfield, Workington, and Swallow Hill (Distington). Other improvements were the provision of a ladies' waiting room at Distington and the enlargement of the offices at Central Station, Workington.

Although the year 1913 showed an increase of mineral revenue to the tune of over £8,000, the Chairman, at the Annual Meeting in February, 1914, pointed out that the previous year had been one in which the coal and railway strikes had occurred.

In the light of later developments, a small "segment" of Mr. J. S. Ainsworth's remark had a prophetic quality. [1] He said, "Two of the main causes of the increase in local taxation are the growing cost of education and the upkeep of the main roads. Owing to the heavy expenditure on them and their capacity for heavy motor traffic the roads are now able to carry a large amount of traffic that used to be carried by the railways." These words were spoken in 1914!

From the outbreak of the War in 1914 right up to the end of the conflict the "Track of the Ironmasters" carried a continuous flow of traffic. [2]

During that period the earnings of the Company were maintained at an average of 4 per cent. Even after the cessation of hostilities the post-war boom in the local iron trade kept the little railway busy right up to its absorption into the London, Midland and Scottish Railway.

Notes to Chapter Two

1.   See Appendix E for brief biographical details of directors of the C&WJR.

2.   The Great War saw the first signs of contraction of the C&WJR system. The heavy traffic generated by the manufacture of munitions and the acute demand for steel, together with the need for more efficient use of limited resources of man-power and equipment, led to many operational rationalisations. From about 1917 the expensive working of mineral trains over the heavily graded Northern Extension was wound down, and traffic was increasingly operated via the M&C and LNWR coastal lines. With only two trains each way a day working through over the Northern Extension by the summer of 1920, closure followed a Board decision of 9 August 1921, that "in view of the pooling scheme introduction, Linefoot Junction and Great Broughton station ... be closed saving £200".

CHAPTER III

DESCRIPTION OF THE LINE

THE Main Line of the Cleator and Workington Junction Railway commences, at its southern end, at Cleator Moor Junction. At this point, 48 chains [1] from Moor Row, the passenger trains in the Up direction left the Rowrah and Marron Junction section of the L. and N. W. and Furness Joint Railways and turned away to the left and northwards. Cleator Moor station, 67 chains from Moor Row, was sited in a shallow cutting a few hundred yards south of the Whitehaven-Cleator main road and about a quarter of a mile from the centre of the town. The commencing gradient is 1 in 264, but, as the track passes under the main road, the gradient steepens to 1 in 71, which persists for nearly a mile followed by a mile and a half of 1 in 70$\frac{1}{2}$. Soon after passing under the Whitehaven road, the River Keekle is crossed by a seven span stone viaduct. Just beyond this point was located the Keekle "halt" platform, where colliers' trains to Walkmill Pit called for the benefit of those miners living at Keekle village (one long row of small houses). During the next mile, the line passes through a rocky cutting and 3 miles and 10 chains from Moor Row reaches Moresby Junction. Here was another "halt" platform (for detraining miners) and the industrial railway from Walkmill Pit comes in on the Down side. There are several stoppage sidings and a "run-round" cross-over. Still climbing, the track passes under the Hensingham (Whitehaven)-Moresby Parks road (having described a shallow "S" curve in the process) and enters Moresby Parks station, 3 miles and 54 chains from Moor Row. Here is a small goods yard and a storage siding. For about half-a-mile the track is "straight and level." Here the C. and W. J. is running along the top of the valley, which runs down from Distington to Parton and Whitehaven, and good views of the sea and the long line of the Scottish Coast across the Solway can be seen on the Up side. The line is hereabouts above the 400-foot level.

After this short, level stretch the gradient steepens abruptly to 1 in 70 down, and, in a series of curves (several of 22 chains radius), falls 200 feet to Distington, 6 miles and 73 chains from Moor Row. About half-a-mile before Distington is reached, the branch from Rowrah comes in on the Up side, having crossed the main line by an overbridge from the east to do so. Distington station is at the extreme north end of the village. The Gilgarran Branch of the L.N.W. and Furness Joint Railway, after passing through Distington Ironworks Yard, came in behind the station (where there was a short platform on the branch) on the Down side. The station also had an additional loop behind the Up platform and several sidings. A stone bridge now carries the line over the main Whitehaven-Workington road, and, immediately beyond, the Distington-Parton section of the Gilgarran branch turned abruptly away to the left and south-westwards. Through Distington there is a short stretch of level track, thereafter steepening to 1 in 94 down as far as Barfs Quarry Siding (on the Up side) and then to 1 in 70 again. The line runs in a shallow cutting and, passing under the Whitehaven-Harrington main road, enters High Harrington station. Here there is a

Cleator Moor Station looking north.

CRA Pattinson Collection
PA0585

15

Distington junction and station looking east about 1960. In the right foreground is the former LNWR and Furness Joint Lines branch to Parton, and to the left branches off the eastern section of that line to Distington Ironworks and Ullock Junction.

CRA Shillcock Collection SHI090

Above
Harrington Junction looking north in 1952. On the left is the cabin which housed the control office, opposite the signal box on the right. The Moss Bay and Derwent branches head left behind the control office.

CRA Dendy Collection DEN095

Right
Workington Central up platform during the making of the feature film "When Stars Look Down" in 1938. The principal stars in the film were Michael Redgrave and Margaret Lockwood.

CRA Pattinson Collection PA0655

Above
View south at Workington Central in May 1951 to the signal box and former locomotive shed, later used as a wagon repair workshop.

CRA Dendy Collection
DEN097

Right
Dock Junction, looking south towards Calva Junction, with the locomotive shed which housed a number of Furness Railway locomotives.

K J Norman Collection

On the Moss Bay branch a United Steel Co. 0-6-0ST takes on water as it nears the summit of its climb towards Harrington Junction. Curving away on the right is the Derwent Branch.

CRA Pattinson Collection
PA0486

Rowrah Branch Junction, looking north towards Distington. The branch on the left climbed up to cross over the main line. The stone building was a former engine shed.

CRA Pattinson Collection PA0532

Left
Cloffocks Junction looking north with a train coming round the curve from Workington Bridge.

CRA Kerr Collection KER189

Right
Distington Junction signals and signal box looking west.
CRA Pattinson Collection PA0636

Moss Bay with the branch climbing away right towards Harrington Junction and the connection into the iron and steel works dropping away to the left. Behind the running line and loop in the foreground the branch continued to Harrington Harbour.
CRA Pattinson Collection PA0490

Harrington Junction. The gradient eases to 1 in 250, followed by a brief level stretch before 1 in 70 is resumed. The marshalling yard is on the Up side, from which the Lowca Light Railway comes in. The ruling gradient of 1 in 70 down continues to Workington (Central), 10 miles and 14 chains from Moor Row. The C. and W. J. engine shed was on the Up side, and there was a fairly extensive goods yard. The Head Offices of the Company were at Workington (Central) Station, which was quite a substantially built stone edifice.

The line beyond Central Station continues in a cutting, dropping sharply at 1 in 70 for 40 chains to Cloffocks Junction, where the spur line to Workington Bridge turned off to the right. A short rise at 1 in 452, steepening again to 1 in 70 carries the track over the River Derwent, across the Workington-Cockermouth line of the L. and N. W. R., and into a shallow cutting to Calva Junction, 10 miles and 59 chains from Moor Row. Here the single track of the Northern Extension line debouched to the right. Beyond Calva Junction, where there is a brief stretch of level running, the line dipped at 1 in 70 down to Dock Junction, 11 miles and 28 chains from Moor Row. The Dock Branch turned sharply off to the left, crossing the Workington-Maryport line of the North-Western by an overbridge just south of St. Helens Colliery and Brickworks. Swinging round on a 10 chains radius curve, it ran southwards and parallel to the L. and N. W .R. to serve Oldside Ironworks and gain access to Lonsdale Dock. The latter was obliterated by the construction of the present United Steel Company's Prince of Wales Dock in 1927. [2] The Dock Branch was just over a mile long. From Dock Junction it was a mere 40 chains, mainly at 1 in 383 down to Siddick Junction. Here are a number of sidings and the C. and W. J. R. passenger trains used to back off the Up platform.

Returning to Calva Junction, the Northern Extension line turned away to the right and north-eastwards, on a rising gradient of 1 in 250 for a brief stretch, followed by a continuous climb at 1 in 70 for $2^1/_2$ miles, broken by a short portion of 1 in 150 just before Seaton. The track followed the high ground north of the Derwent Valley and, from beyond Camerton Colliery, ran mainly level, broken by portions of 1 in 540 up to Great Broughton, 15 miles and 63 chains from Moor Row. Between Seaton and Great Broughton the Northern Extension served Buckhill Colliery, of the Allerdale Coal Company, 14 miles and 68 chains from Moor Row. From Great Broughton the track descended for two miles, first at 1 in 250 and then 1 in 83 to Linefoot Junction on the M. and C. Derwent Branch, 17 miles and 9 chains from Moor Row.

At Linefoot were a number of storage sidings for accommodating traffic, mainly East Coast coke inwards and Scottish Iron traffic outwards, as well as landsale coal from pits on the Northern Extension itself. There were a number of sharp curves on the section, including two of 10 chains radius just beyond Calva Junction and one of 15 chains approaching Linefoot.

Note to Chapter Three

1.   A chain is a measurement of distance equal to 22 yards. Hence one chain is 20.18 metres; 48 chains is 0.6 mile, 1056 yards, 969 metres or 0.97 kilometres.

2.   Since about 1981 the dock has been owned and managed by Cumbria County Council.

The railways always dressed for ceremonial occasions, here at Workington Central for the Coronation of King Edward VII and Queen Alexandra. The great event was scheduled to take place on 26 June 1902, but had to be postponed only two days beforehand because the King suffered an acute attack of appendicitis. The Coronation eventually took place on 9 August.

CRA Collection

CHAPTER IV

"BAIRD'S LINE"

TO ALL C. and W. J.R. employees, the Company's principal branch line, from Distington (Rowrah Branch) Junction to Rowrah, was known as "Baird's Line." [1] The interlocking interests of the West Cumbrian and Scottish ironmasters gives the first clue to this title. The big firm of Glasgow iron founders, Messrs. William Baird and Company, not only "imported" haematite pig iron from West Cumberland, but also obtained mining rights in the area. In 1875 this firm obtained powers to construct a railway from Rowrah, on the then Whitehaven, Cleator and Egremont Railway, to Kelton and Knockmurton, a distance of 3¹/₂ miles. Known as the Rowrah and Kelton Fell (Mineral) Railway, it served several iron ore mines and a large limestone quarry. Since one of the R. and K. F. (M.) R. directors was also on the C. and W. J. Board (Mr. Robert Alleyne Robinson), it was not surprising to learn that the construction of the Distington-Rowrah Branch was "tied-up" with the building of the R. and K. F. (M.) R. [2] The unpopularity of the W. C. and E. with local ironmasters about this period, owing to the increases in freight charges, has already been touched on earlier in this book, so the success of "Baird's Line" seemed reasonably assured from the outset.

The following gentlemen, all directors of Messrs. William Baird and Company, were also directors of the Rowrah and Kelton Fell line, and their names will be familiar to most railway enthusiasts: James Baird, Alexander Whitelaw, and Andrew K. McCosh. There was also another "tie-up" with Harrington Ironworks, which drew the bulk (of its supplies of limestone for furnace flux) from Salter Quarry on the Kelton Fell railway. Further details of the R. and K. F.(M.) R. will be found at the end of this chapter. [3]

Returning to "Baird's Line," this left the main line, on the Down side, climbing sharply at 1 in 70, and, by a climbing turn, crossed over the main line in an easterly direction. With two sharp curves of 10 and 15 chains radius the gradient steepened to 1 in 44 for just over two miles up to Oatlands. Here was situated the colliery of that name worked by the Moresby Coal Company. A single "halt" platform was provided here to serve the pit and the nearby village of Pica. Just before reaching the pit the line ran in quite a deep rock cutting, passing under the Moresby-Pica-Lamplugh road. Beyond Oatlands the gradient eased momentarily to 1 in 990 up, followed by 1 in 52 up, and over the shoulder of the intervening moorland. Here the branch reached a height of 600 feet above sea level: the highest point on the "Track of the Ironmasters." From here there is a magnificent view of the Lake District fells in the Ennerdale and Loweswater areas, while, to seaward, are the hills on the Scottish side of the Solway Firth and the Isle of Man.

From the summit of the branch the line swings down the side of the intervening valley, mostly at 1 in 60, and crosses the "floor" of the latter on a high embankment on a 14 chains radius curve, known locally as "Brownrigg's Curve." From here the metals climbed again, at 1 in 64, for nearly a mile.

A deep rock cutting then took "Baird's Line" under the Egremont-Cockermouth main road, from whence the line dropped at 1 in 80 to Arlecdon (6 miles from Rowrah Branch Junction). Here was a station and small goods yard. Another half-mile carried the line over the Cleator Moor-Marron Junction section of the L. and N. W. and Furness Joint Railway. Here "Baird's Line" turned north to make an end-on junction with the Rowrah and Kelton Fell line, parallel to the "Joint Line," with which connection could also be made by a "back-shunt." A branch also went direct into the Rowrah Head and Rowrah Hall limestone quarries of the Workington Iron and Steel Company. [4]

When first opened, the Rowrah Branch dealt with mineral traffic only. This consisted of coal from Oatlands Colliery and iron ore and limestone picked up at Rowrah quarries and from the R. and K. F. (M.) R. at Rowrah. In later years an afternoon and evening passenger train from Arlecdon to Workington and back was put on twice a week – on Wednesdays and Saturdays. During the 1914-18 War this service was cancelled but restored again on Saturdays only for a short time afterwards. In addition, an early morning and evening trip was run for pitmen between Arlecdon and Oatlands. This was worked by the Moresby Coal Company. [5]

Oatlands Station looking north with wagons waiting in the colliery sidings.

CRA Pattinson Collection PA0547

Rowrah Junction with the line to Rowrah Hall Quarry in the foreground in January 1966. To the right the line proceeds to an end-on junction with the R&KFR (see next picture). The line formerly climbed away to cross over the former Whitehaven, Cleator & Egremont Railway, and the climb continues past Arlecdon station in the distance.

F W Shuttleworth

Rowrah Junction looking north in January 1966 with the line of the former Whitehaven, Cleator & Egremont Railway on the left. The Rowrah & Kelton Fell Railway formerly continued beyond the buffer stops in the distance.

F W Shuttleworth

The mineral trips (two or three each way between Distington and Rowrah, with an extra each way between Distington and Oatlands for coal traffic) were worked by the C. and W. J. Company's own engines.

After the 1923 amalgamation and the withdrawal from stock of the C. and W. J. locomotives, traffic on the branch was entrusted to L. M. S. "standard 3F" 0-6-0 tanks. Oatlands Colliery was worked out in the early 1930s, but limestone traffic from the Rowrah quarries continued to be worked over "Baird's Line" until 1939, [6] when the L. M. S. decided to work it round by Marron Junction. Therefore, in that year, the whole of the track except for a short section from Rowrah towards Arlecdon – long enough to cover the "back-shunt" necessary to run into the limestone quarries from the "wrong end," as it were, of "Baird's Line" – was removed. To-day, the solitary freight which works up to Rowrah from Moor Row, via Frizington, collects the loaded limestone wagons from the quarries, works them to Marron Junction, where they are placed in a siding for onward working to Workington. Empties are collected from Marron sidings by the same working and deposited at Rowrah before the "roadside" trundles back to Moor Row. [7]

The construction of the R. and K. F. (M.) R. was completed in 1877. It left the Whitehaven, Cleator and Egremont Railway at a point 360 yards west of Rowrah station. On the completion of "Baird's Line," an end-on junction was made with the latter at Rowrah, the connection with the W. C. and E. R. being relegated to a "back-shunt" link. At Sheriff Gate, about half-a-mile from Rowrah, two branches left the "main line." One turned south to serve the Salter limestone quarry and iron mines, which were worked by the Harrington Iron Company, the other turned north and later passed under the R. and K. F. (M.) R. to serve Stockhow Limestone Quarry. The main line passed through Kirkland village (where a small coal and goods depot was provided) and continued for $3^{1}/_{2}$ miles to serve the Knockmurton and Kelton Fell iron mines, standing 580 feet above sea-level at the foot of Hare Ghyll, above Ennerdale Lake. [8]

The line earned steady dividends down to the end of the 19th century, but by 1910, the ore deposits showed signs of exhaustion, and it was mainly limestone traffic which kept the Company going. After the 1914-18 War, Messrs. Bairds, who had been anxious to dispose of the line for some time, sold it to the Whitehaven Haematite Iron Company, at Cleator Moor, for £750. The latter concern also provided a further £600 to put the line, as far as Salter Quarry, into a reasonable state of repair. In 1920 the Cleator Moor Ironworks were purchased by the North Lonsdale Iron Company and closed down. This sent the Salter Quarry into liquidation. Finally, in 1933, the railway was purchased by Mr. J. W. Kitchen, of Moor Row, and dismantled the year after. [9]

The Rowrah and Kelton Fell Railway was worked by train staff and ticket. There was a signal box at Sheriff Gate, the signals being of the lattice girder type. These, and the boards protecting the junction with the C. and W. J. R. and the "Joint Line" at Rowrah No. 1 signalbox, were maintained by the L. and N. W. R. linesman, and the wages of the signalman at Rowrah No. 1 box (who was a Furness employee) were paid by the R. and K. F. (M.) R.

Traffic from the iron mines was usually worked by ex-W. C. and E. saddle tanks, particularly No. 108A and 98A. During the last years of the Salter Quarry section's active life two Manning Wardle 0-6-0 tanks, named "Wyndham" and "Dinah," worked the traffic. They had been used originally as contractor's locomotives during the construction of the "Track of the Ironmasters." There was also a Barclay 0-4-0 saddle tank, built in 1881, named "Salter." Originally supplied to the Wyndham Mining Company, at Egremont, it was sold by Mr. Kitchen to the Whitehaven Colliery Company and ended its days shunting coal on Whitehaven Harbour. [10]

In 1882 the share capital of the R. and K. F. (M.) R. was increased by £9,000 (raised by Board of Trade Certificate), and a Bill was prepared for "an extension to Ennerdale, and for other purposes," but this was never proceeded with. Probably the Company had in mind the further exploitation of ore deposits in the region, which further boring operations proved to be uneconomic.

Notes to Chapter Four

1.   The term "Baird's Line" appears nowhere in official records. The term would more obviously apply to the Rowrah & Kelton Fell Railway which was promoted and owned by Baird's, the Scottish ironmasters, than to the C&WJR branch from Distington to Rowrah which connected with it.

2.   The two main traffic sources which the Rowrah Branch was intended to serve were the Rowrah & Kelton Fell (Mineral) Railway and Oatlands Colliery of the Moresby Coal Company. Both companies contributed towards the costs of the parliamentary processes to obtain the Act authorising construction of the branch. It is possible that this involvement led to the "Baird's Line" reference. Oatlands Colliery was sunk in 1880, worked until 1932, and was finally abandoned in 1934. The Moresby Coal Co. was taken over by the United Steel Companies Ltd. in 1924.

3.   Names which perhaps were more familiar to readers of fifty years ago than in the early years of the 21st century. The following explanations may help modern readers.

James Baird (*b. 5 December 1802, d. 20 June 1876*): ironmaster and coal owner, joint proprietor, with his father, William, and brothers, of Gartsherrie Ironworks at Coatbridge, ten miles east of Glasgow, managing the business from 1830; from 1850 to 1876 he was M.P. for Falkirk Burghs. William Baird & Co. acquired its first interests in West Cumberland iron mining in 1869 when the company took a lease for mining at Knockmurton, near Lamplugh, extending its interests a couple of years later when it leased mining rights at Kelton.

Alexander Whitelaw (*b. 1823, d. 1 July 1879*) was one-time manager of Gartsherrie Ironworks, and from 1860 a partner in William Baird & Co. He was a Conservative M.P. for Glasgow from 1874 to 1879. A nephew of James Baird, he was father of the better known William Whitelaw and great-grandfather of William Whitelaw, M.P. for Penrith and the Border (*b. 28 June 1918, d. 1 July 1999*, Deputy Prime Minister 1983-1988, created viscount, 1983).

Alexander's son, William Whitelaw (*b. 15 March 1868, d. 19 January 1946)*, was a director of the Highland Railway (from 1898 to 1912, chairman 1902 to 1912), a director of the North British Railway (from 1908 to 1922, latterly chairman), and chairman of the London & North Eastern Railway from 1923 to 1938. He was also a director of the Bank of Scotland. His name, *William Whitelaw,* was first bestowed on one of the original LNER class A1 4-6-2 locomotives, No. 2563, built in 1924, later to become Class A3 No. 64 *Tagalie* (B.R. No. 60064, withdrawn 1961). On 24 July 1941 the name *William Whitelaw* was transferred at York to Class A4 4-6-2 No. 4492. This locomotive had been built in 1937 and originally named *Great Snipe*; it later became LNER No. 4, then British Railways No. 60004 and was withdrawn from service in 1966.

Andrew Kirkwood McCosh managed Baird's West Cumberland interests in the 1870s, later becoming a director of William Baird & Co. His son, also Andrew K. McCosh (*b. 31 August 1880, d. 27 September 1967*),

mining engineer, was also a director of the North British Railway up to 1922, and of the LNER throughout its lifetime from 1923 to 1947. From 1929 until 1947 he was chairman of the company's Locomotive Committee. LNER Class A4 4-6-2 locomotive No. 4494 (built 1937 and originally named *Osprey)* was renamed *Andrew K. McCosh* at a ceremony at Kings Cross station on 29 October 1942. It later became LNER No. 3 and then British Railways No. 60003, being withdrawn from service in 1962.

4.   Rowrah Head quarry had previously been served by the Whitehaven, Cleator & Egremont Railway; Rowrah Hall was a later development by the Workington Iron & Steel Company from about 1921, when the "Rowrah New Limestone Siding" was installed. See also notes to Chapter VIII.

5.   Details of the locomotives of the Moresby Coal Company are given in the notes to Chapter VIII.

6.   The Rowrah Branch actually closed from 8 August 1938.

7.   The limestone traffic from Rowrah to Workington, routed via Moor Row, continued for another 25 years from the date when McGowan Gradon was writing. Working of Rowrah Hall Quarry (then owned by the British Steel Corporation) ceased in March 1978 and the railway to Rowrah was lifted in September 1980.

8.   There is a very complex history of proposals for railways to tap the iron ore resources in and around Ennerdale. The first of several proposals for a railway from Rowrah to serve the new iron mines at Kelton Fell and beyond was put forward in 1871 by John Hoskins, a local surveyor. This would have been a three-foot gauge line and was intended to run high above the north side of Ennerdale, skirting round the flanks of Banna Fell, to reach ore veins at Floutern Tarn. Further schemes followed during the 1870s and 80s, details of which are discussed in *Cumbrian Railways* and other published works.

W. Baird & Co. initially approached the Whitehaven, Cleator & Egremont Railway with a view to persuading the latter company to build a branch to serve the iron mines at Kelton Fell. The WC&ER board, however, refused, saying it would not provide sufficient return on the capital investment required. This led Bairds to sponsor a separate company to build its own standard-gauge line from Rowrah. The Rowrah & Kelton Fell (Mineral) Railway was authorised on 16 July 1874 with a capital of £30,000. Its initial directors were Robert Alleyne Robinson (see Appendix E), Alexander Brogden, James Baird, Alexander Whitelaw, William Wallace and Martin Boundy who was replaced by Andrew Kirkwood McCosh in 1878, later becoming chairman. The contract for construction was awarded to Harrison Hodgson of Workington and the line was ready for opening on 11 November 1876, the actual opening being delayed by a legal dispute with the WC&ER. Opening in mid-January 1877, Bairds contracted to supply the motive power in the form of an 0-4-0 saddle tank, numbered 13 in their own series, and named *Kelton Fell*

An LMS 3F 0-6-0 rounding Brownrigg's Curve at the start of the long climb to Steel Brow. The load of limestone hoppers from Rowrah Hall Quarry is bound for the Workington Iron & Steel Works.
CRA Pattinson Collection PA0569

(see note 10 below), in return for half of the gross receipts from traffic and other sources.

In 1884 the directors of the Rowrah & Kelton Fell Railway Co. were:

J. William Weir, chairman, 168 West George Street, Glasgow;
Robert Alleyne Robinson;
Andrew Kirkwood McCosh, Gartsherrie, Coatbridge,
John Alexander, Gartsherrie;
William Weir, Crookedholme, Kilmarnock.

9.   The R&KFR was purchased jointly by the Whitehaven Hematite Iron Co. and the Salter & Eskett Park Mining Co. in 1920 and operated by them, using the Salter Company's locomotives. In the same year the Cleator Moor ironworks of the Whitehaven Company were taken over the North Lonsdale Iron Company Ltd. of Ulverston which kept the works in operation until 1929. They were finally dismantled in 1934 and an industrial estate now occupies their former site. For details of locomotives see Chapter VIII.

10.   Traffic on the R&KFR from its opening was worked by the company's own locomotive, an 0-4-0 saddle tank built by Neilsen & Co. of Glasgow (works no. 2203 of 1876) and named *Kelton Fell*. This engine operated from its small shed at Sheriff Gate until 1914 when it was transferred away to Baird's Gartsherrie Ironworks at Coatbridge. It is now preserved by the Scottish Railway Preservation Society at Bo'ness, near Falkirk. It appears probable that C&WJR locomotives then worked the small remaining traffic on the line until 1918, not the ex-WC&ER locos referred to by Gradon. After the take-over of the line by the Salter Mining and Whitehaven Hematite Iron Cos. In 1920, traffic was worked by the Salter Company's locomotives

to Rowrah Junction. These were probably the locos *Wyndham, Dinah* and *Salter* mentioned by Gradon, though only *Dinah* was a Manning Wardle. Whether the first two of these were the same locos used by Robert Ward & Co., the contractor for construction of the C&WJR main line and the Rowrah Branch, remains an unsolved question.

There are many questions also about the locomotives of the Salter Mining Co. Ltd. The following is a tentative list only:

WYNDHAM
0-4-0T with outside cylinders; built by Fletcher, Jennings at Lowca, works no. 178 of 1880; acquired from Wyndham Mining Co., Egremont, date uncertain, probably scrapped on site.

SALTER
0-4-0ST with outside cylinders; built by Barclays & Co., Riverside Works, Kilmarnock, works no. 270 of 1880; acquired from Wyndham Mining Co., Egremont after 1907; disposed of to William Pit, Whitehaven in 1927.

MOUNTAINEER
0-4-0ST with outside cylinders; built by Dick & Stephenson, Airdrie; origin and disposal unknown.

DINAH (?)
0-6-0ST with inside cylinders; built by Manning Wardle & Co. Ltd., Hunslet, Leeds; recorded here in 1928-9 but other details uncertain; scrapped at Cleator Moor about 1938.

Un-named
0-6-0ST with inside cylinders; built by Manning Wardle & Co. Ltd., Hunslet, Leeds; recorded here around 1928-9 but other details uncertain; probably scrapped on site.

CHAPTER V

THE LOWCA LIGHT RAILWAY

MAKING an end-on junction with the branch from Harrington Junction, at Rosehill Junction (1 mile 31 chains long) was the Lowca Light Railway. This single line, the property of the Workington Iron and Steel Company Limited (later the United Steel Company Ltd.), is 2 miles and 4 chains in length. It was constructed to connect the collieries and by-product plant at Lowca and the brickworks at Micklam with the blast furnaces at Workington. [1]

The track follows the edge of the high ground above the cliffs along the seashore between Harrington and Parton and is steeply graded throughout. The table of gradients given below will give some idea of the contours of the Lowca Light Railway. [2]

Harrington to Lowca

M.C.	M.C.			
0.0	0.5	Rising	1 in 150	Harrington Junction – Rose Hill
0.5	0.17	,,	1 in 70	,, ,, ,,
0.17	0.20	Level	–	,, ,, ,,
0.20	0.75	Falling	1 in 100	,, ,, ,,
0.75	1.31	Level	–	Rose Hill – Copperas Hill
0.0	0.13	Rising	1 in 17	,, ,,
0.13	0.16	,,	1 in 26	,, ,,
0.16	0.28	,,	1 in 49	Copperas Hill – Micklam
0.28	0.40	,,	1 in 103	,, ,,
0.40	0.46	,,	1 in 420	,, ,,
0.46	0.54	,,	1 in 68	,, ,,
0.54	0.64	,,	1 in 35	,, ,,
0.64	0.78	,,	1 in 37	,, ,,
0.78	1.11	,,	1 in 44	,, ,,
1.11	1.16	,,	1 in 94	,, ,,
1.16	1.28	Falling	1 in 78	,, ,,
1.28	1.41	,,	1 in 94	,, ,,
1.41	1.54	,,	1 in 171	,, ,,
1.54	1.60	,,	1 in 56	Micklam – Lowca
1.60	1.64	,,	1 in 37	,, ,,
1.64	1.74	,,	1 in 55	,, ,,
1.74	1.79	,,	1 in 40	,, ,,
1.79	2.4	,,	1 in 70	Lowca

Mineral traffic over the Lowca Light Railway, consisting of coal, coke, tar, and sundry by-products, was worked by the locomotives and men of the Workington Iron and Steel Company, and consisted of about four to half-a-dozen booked trips in each direction. After running over their own track these trains reached Workington over either the Moss Bay or Derwent branches of the C. and W. J. R., according to the plants for which their loads were destined.

In addition to the above-mentioned mineral workings the C. and W. J. provided a "3rd Class only" passenger service from Workington to Lowca, mainly for the benefit of miners working at Lowca Collieries. One train, the first to reach Lowca in the early morning, started from Seaton on the Northern Extension and an afternoon one – except on Saturdays – and a mid-day one on Saturdays only, ran back to Seaton. Shortly before the 1914-18 War, in July 1913, the following service of passenger trains was in operation on week-days only:

Rosehill loop, platform and token hut, seen looking north east in 1962.

M J Andrews

Rosehill Junction with a loaded train headed by a United Steel Co. 0-6-0ST. The former mineral line to Harrington Harbour headed down in front of the houses at a gradient of about 1 in 15.

M J Andrews

On the 1 in 17 of Copperas Hill a pair of the United Steel Companies' Yorkshire Engine Co.-built 0-4-0 diesels, Nos. 207 and 210, head for Lowca on 7 September 1968.

Peter W Robinson

DOWN TRAINS

		am	SO pm	SE	SO	SE	X	X
SEATON	dep.	5-05	——	——	2 05	3 40	——	——
Workington	„	5 15	1220	1 15	2 12	3 47	4 15	9 15
Rosehill (Archer Street Halt)	„	5 22	1227	1 22	——	——	4 22	9 22
Copperas Hill	„	5 25	1230	1 25	——	——	4 25	9 25
Micklam	„	5 35	1240	1 35	——	——	4 35	9 35
LOWCA	arr.	5 40	1245	1 40	——	——	4 40	9 40

UP TRAINS

		am	SO pm	SE	SE	SO		
LOWCA	dep.	6 10	1 15	2 50	4 55	5 15	1015	.....
Micklam	„	6 15	1 20	2 55	5 00	5 20	1020	.....
Copperas Hill	„	6 25	1 30	3 05	5 10	5 30	1030	.....
Rosehill (Archer Street Halt)	„	6 28	1 37	3 08	5 13	5 33	1033	.....
Workington	„	6 35	1 45	3 15	5 20	5 40	1040	.....
SEATON	arr.	——	1 57	3 32	——	5 52	——	.....

SO – Saturdays only.   SE – Saturdays excepted.   X – 15 minutes later on Saturday.

The Lowca Light Railway was worked by the Electric Train Tablet System, and signal cabins were provided at Rosehill and Lowca. There were also Ground Frames for releasing the siding points at Copperas Hill and Micklam Brickworks. These were unlocked by the tablet of Annett's Key (Bank staff).

From Lowca all mineral trains were banked at the rear up to Copperas Hill and from Rosehill Junction to Copperas Hill or Lowca. In the Up direction all mineral trains were brought to a dead stand at Copperas Hill stop signal, which acted as a repeater to the home signal at Harrington Junction. Here brakes were pinned down before proceeding. [3]

The passenger train engines (usually Furness "Sharpies") carried the conventional lamps for passenger or empty stock trains, but the U. S. C.-worked minerals carried twin lamps either side of the chimney base for mineral trains and a single one over the left buffer for light engine, light engines coupled together, or engine and brake.

In 1918 an additional "halt" station was opened at Harrington (Church Road) between Rosehill and Harrington Junction. The service on the Lowca Light Railway in the winter of 1919 was as follows

UP TRAINS

		am	SO pm	SE	SE	SO	SO	SE	SO
LOWCA	dep.	6 10	1 05	1 30	2 30	——	5 35	9 00	——	1015
Micklam	„	6 12	1 07	1 32	2 32	——	——	9 02	——	1017
Copperas Hill	„	6 17	1 12	1 37	2 37	——	——	9 07	——	1022
Rosehill (Archer Street Halt)	„	6 20	1 15	1 40	2 40	——	5 42	9 10	——	1025
Church Road	„	6 22	1 19	1 42	2 42	——	5 49	9 12	——	1027
WORKINGTON	arr.	6 29	1 27	1 49	2 49	——	5 54	9 18	——	1034
WORKINGTON..................	dep.	——	——	——	——	4 30	——	——	9 15	——
SEATON	arr.	——	——	——	——	4 37	——	——	9 22	——

				SO am	SE am	SE pm	SO	SE	SO
SEATON .... dep.	——	——	——	——	4 55	——	——	9 30
WORKINGTON .... arr.	——	——	——	——	5 02	——	——	9 37
WORKINGTON .... dep.	5 10	1130	1240	2 00	5 05	8 30	8 40	9 40
Church Road .... „	5 17	1137	1247	2 07	5 12	8 37	8 47	9 47
Rosehill (Archer Street Halt) .... „	5 19	1139	1249	2 09	5 14	8 39	8 50	9 50
Copperas Hill .... „	5 22	1142	1252	2 12	——	8 42	——	9 52
Micklam .... „	5 27	1147	1257	2 17	——	8 47	——	9 57
LOWCA ....arr.	5 29	1149	1259	2 19	5 20	8 49	——	9 59

SO – Saturdays only. SE – Saturdays excepted.

It will be noted that by this time the daily through run to and from Seaton had been abolished, and the passenger service over the Northern Extension was confined to a couple of "Saturdays only" trips to and from Workington in the afternoon and evening of that day.

After the abandoning of the passenger service over the Light Railway the stations on the branch line were demolished and the signal boxes on the line closed thus reducing the status of the L. L. R. to a purely industrial railway, as which it runs today. [4]

Mention must be made of the very steeply graded line which ran down to Harrington Harbour from Rosehill Junction. This was used to convey coal from Lowca Colliery for shipment from Harrington. The gradient was about 1 in 15, and three empty wagons up from the harbour was the limit for the small industrial locomotives handling the traffic. On more than one occasion wagons and locomotives "ran away" on the down gradient and finished up in Harrington Dock ! By reversal on the dockside, entry into Harrington Ironworks could be made, but ore and coke traffic to these furnaces was worked round by the Moss Bay branch of the C. and W. J. with its easier gradients. With the silting up of Harrington Harbour in the late 1920s the use of the branch was abandoned, although the track is still in situ. [5]

Lowca with Furness Railway 0-6-0 "Sharpie" No 92 of 1874, ready to leave on the first day of the workers' service to Workington on 2 June 1913. *CRA Kerr Collection KER314*

A United Steel Co. 0-6-0ST built by Robert Stephenson & Co. nears Micklam with a train mainly of hopper wagons from the Workington works in the late 1930s.   *CRA Pattinson Collection PA0483*

Notes on Chapter Five

1.   The Lowca Light Railway had a much longer history than Gradon implies here. The mining rights in this area were owned by the Curwen family of Workington Hall. As they opened a series of mines above Harrington and Lowca they built a tramway as early as 1760 to link them to Harrington Harbour which descended from Copperas Hill at grades as steep as 1 in 15/17. This was a wooden-railed, horse-worked waggonway. By the 1840s it may have become disused. The ironworks on the seashore at Harrington was built in 1857, but was not at first successful. In 1863 it was taken over by the Scottish partnership of Messrs. Bain, Blair and Patterson who also leased mining rights in the Harrington-Lowca area, to become known as the "Harrington Colliery". They also took over and renewed the waggonway and extended it to the new pits at Lowca. The C&WJR branch, from Harrington Junction, which made a junction with the former waggonway part-way up the steepest part of the gradient at Rosehill, was opened in July 1879. In 1901 brickmaking was started at Micklam, Harrington No. 10 pit was sunk in 1910 and the adjacent Koppers coke ovens completed in 1911. The shortage of housing and labour at Lowca led to a request to the C&WJR for a workmen's service from Workington, and this commenced from 15 April 1912, worked by Workington Iron & Steel Co. locomotives. Almost immediately the Company considered there was scope for running a public service, and an application was submitted for a Light Railway Order to permit this. After a Public Inquiry in Workington on 20 July 1912, the Order was signed on 16 May 1913, with the new public service commencing from 2 June 1913, worked now by Furness Railway locomotives (see *Cumbrian Railways* Vol. 7 No. 2 [May 2001] pp. 20-24).

2.   The climb to Copperas Hill, with its 1 in 17 gradient, is believed to have been the steepest adhesion-operated gradient in Great Britain over which passenger services were regularly worked.

3.   The signal at Copperas Hill was more likely to have been an outer or repeater home for Rosehill Junction.

4.   Operation of the Lowca Light Railway, and the associated Moss Bay and Harrington branches of the C&WJR continued for several years after the closure and lifting of the Cleator and Workington main line (see Appendix A for full details of closure dates). By-products from the Moss Bay coke ovens were brought to the by-product works at Lowca for distillation and treatment, and coal was carried from the Harrington Collieries at Lowca to the iron and steel works for coking. Even after the last of the Harrington Collieries, No. 10, closed in July 1968, the washery was retained to treat coal from the Solway Colliery at Workington, the coal being carried to Lowca via the Whitehaven Junction line to Parton, then up the remains of the Whitehaven, Cleator & Egremont Railway's Whitehaven branch to No. 4 Pit Siding, from where National Coal Board locomotive would complete the haul to Lowca. Treated coal would then taken to the coking plant over the Lowca Light Railway. Solway Colliery closed in May 1973, and the Lowca Light Railway closed from the 23rd, the last train being run on the 26th for members of the Border Railway Society.

5.   The rails of the Harrington Harbour Branch could still be seen in the early 1950s when Gradon was writing this history; now, in 2004, they are long since gone.

CHAPTER VI

THE LOCOMOTIVES

IN my book, *Furness Railway, its Rise and Development, 1846-1923,* I dealt briefly with the locomotives owned by the C. and W. J. R. Since the publication of that book – in 1946 – it has been possible to obtain further and fuller information and to correct certain errors which crept into the first list. [1]

It should be explained that, initially, the Furness Railway only worked the C. and W. J. main line from Cleator Moor Junction to Siddick Junction (and later the Northern Extension from Calva Junction to Linefoot). When the Rowrah, Moss Bay and Derwent Branches were constructed the C. and W. J. purchased their own engines to work these lines, all of which were dealing with mineral traffic only.

For three of their first four locomotives the Cleator Company patronised a local firm, the famous Lowca Foundry of Messrs. Fletcher, Jennings and Company, of Parton, near Whitehaven.

The first engine ordered was an 0-4-0 tank engine (No. 187 in Messrs. Fletcher, Jennings' list) with outside cylinders 14 by 20 inches in diameter, and a working pressure of 130 lbs. Like all the engines owned by the Company she was named after one of the directors' residences, in this instance "Brigham Hill," the home of Mr. W. Fletcher, the chairman. In order to deal with the chaldron-type wagons then used to convey iron ore from the local mines, "Brigham Hill" was fitted with "clog" buffers. She had a "partly closed" cab, with spectacles fore and aft; two three-inch Ashcroft lubicators; shackles, and hook at the end of a chain instead of the usual "drag hooks" and a red and white tender lamp. Delivered in 1881, she soon distinguished herself by regularly hauling six loaded wagons, weighing some 75 tons, up the two miles long 1 in 44 climb from Distington to Oatlands, which abounded in sharp curves, and blowing off steam the whole way. She was withdrawn in 1894.

Records of the second engine, obtained from Lowca, are scanty. Named "Rothersyke," after the home of Mr. R. Jefferson, Egremont, she was another 0-4-0 tank of similar dimensions to "Brigham Hill," and may have been a second-hand purchase, since there is no record of an engine of that name in Messrs. Fletcher, Jennings' list.

Increasing train weights soon demanded more powerful locomotives to move them and, in 1884, a six-coupled saddle tank engine was obtained from Messrs. Robert Stephenson and Company. She had inside cylinders, 17 by 24 inches, and was given the name "South Lodge," the residence of Mr. R. Alleyne Robinson. Three years later a similar engine was ordered from Lowca. This was "Harecroft" (Mr. J. S. Ainsworth's mansion at Gosforth). On August 8th, 1887, she carried out her trials in the presence of Messrs. Prior and Taylor, of the C. and W. J. and Messrs. Cursdell and Hughes, of the Lowca Foundry.

The "test train" consisted of 12 loaded iron ore wagons with a gross weight of 188 tons, plus a $10^1/_2$ -ton brake van and the engine herself weighing (partly full) about $43^1/_2$ tons. The total weight of 242 tons was "taken easily" at 15 m.p.h. up the ruling gradient of 1 in 70 from Moor Row to Moresby Parks, a distance of about three miles.

Steam pressure at the start of the run was 145 lbs. and rose gradually to 152 lbs., but owing to the defective closing of the Salter spring balance safety valves, it fell back to 132 lbs. The injector was on throughout the trip. "Good, round coal" from Walkmill Colliery, Moresby, was used, and the track was stated to be in good order, with fine weather and a dry rail.

Robert Stephenson and Company supplied another six-coupled saddle tank in 1890. This was "Moresby Hall" (home of Mr. William Burnyeat). She was similar to "South Lodge". Stephenson's also supplied a new "Brigham Hill" in 1894 to replace the four-coupled Fletcher, Jennings engine. The new engine was another 0-6-0 saddle tank with the same dimensions as her older sisters. The name of the home of Mr. W. B. Turner, "Ponsonby Hall," was given to the last 0-6-0 tank supplied by Stephenson's – in 1896.

C&WJR No. 3 "South Lodge". No. 3 was built by Robert Stephenson & Co in Newcastle in 1884 and served until 1920. It was named after the home of director Robert Alleyne Robinson near Cockermouth. CRA Collection

C&WJR No. 7 "Ponsonby Hall". Built in 1896 by Robert Stephenson & Co. and named after the residence near Gosforth of William Barrow Turner, it was withdrawn by the LMS in December 1926.

CRA Collection

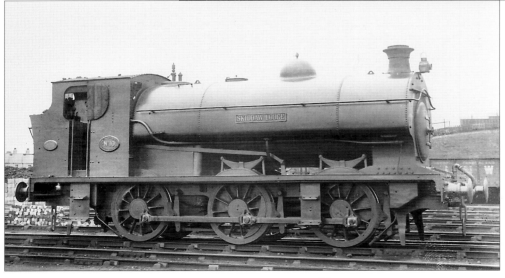

CWJR No. 10 "Skiddaw Lodge". Built by Peckett & Co. of Bristol in 1920, it was sold by the LMS in 1932 to Hartley Main Colliery in Northumberland. Skiddaw Lodge, near Keswick, was the home of company director Joseph Ellis.

CRA Collection

In 1907 "South Lodge" was withdrawn from traffic and her place in the list was filled by a new 0-6-0 saddle tank engine supplied by Peckett, of Bristol. This locomotive, named "Hutton Hall," had cylinders 18 by 24 inches, and wheels 4ft. 6ins. in diameter; an extra 6 inches compared with the Stephenson products. Her wheelbase was 14 feet and the water capacity of her saddle tank 1,400 gallons. She weighed $50^1/_2$ tons. Peckett's supplied her sister, "Millgrove," in 1919. The latter replaced "Harecroft," which was sold to the Lowca No. 10 colliery of the United Steel Company. Also in 1919, Hudswell Clarke, of Leeds, supplied a dimensionally similar engine in "Skiddaw Lodge." She replaced "Moresby Hall," which was scrapped.

These foregoing ten locomotives comprised the total motive power operated by the Cleator and Workington Junction Railway from the opening of the line down to the 1923 amalgamation. In addition to carrying their names on a brass plate on the tank sides, numbers were also carried on a circular brass plaque on the cab sides. Domes of all the engines were of polished brass and the connecting rods were painted vermilion. The livery was black, lined out in red.

When the London, Midland and Scottish Railway came into being in 1923 the "Track of the Ironmasters" was absorbed into it. Five locomotives were then running and were re-numbered from 11564 to 11568. `11564 (formerly No. 6, "Brigham Hill") was the first to be withdrawn – on December 11th 1926; 11565 (No. 8, "Hutton Hall") went on December 3rd, 1927, and 11565 (No. 7, "Ponsonby Hall") followed one week later. No. 9, "Millgrove," as L. M. S. 11567, ran until May 12th 1928. All these locomotives were cut up on being withdrawn from stock. Finally, there only remained "Skiddaw Lodge" (C. and W. J. No. 10 and L. M. S. No. 11568). She ran on her native heath until June 22nd, 1932, when the L. M. S. sold her to a Whitehaven firm of contractors, Messrs. R. Fraser and Company. This firm disposed of her to the Hartley Main Collieries, in County Durham, where she is still working, now under the banner of the N.C.B.

Since the Furness Railway supplied the motive power for the major portion of the C. and W. J. system the locomotives employed by the working company deserve some mention.

History proves that in almost every instance when a larger railway has worked the lines of a smaller one the engines provided for the job have rarely been the cream of the working company's stud. In this regard the Furness was no breaker with tradition. Engines relegated from main line duties between Carnforth, Barrow, and Whitehaven, especially goods classes, as well as locomotives of the erstwhile Whitehaven, Cleator and Egremont Railway (from 1879 known as the L. and N. W. and Furness Joint Railway) usually gravitated to the Moor Row or Siddick sheds. The Moor Row depot, of course, also supplied engines for working the "Joint Lines," but any engine shedded there was also liable for duties over the "Track of the Ironmasters."

Since the whole of the locomotive stud of the Furness Railway has been fully dealt with in my book on that system, it will be sufficient here to mention only those engines, which were C. and W. J. "regulars," rarely straying from within its borders, except when due at Barrow for heavy overhaul, beyond the capacity of the Moor Row Shops.

Probably those engines most closely identified with the line were that sturdy bunch of ex-W. C. and E. 0-6-0 saddle tanks, Nos. 100A, 101A, 107A, 109A, and 112A. Rarely were they absent from duties between Cleator Moor and Siddick. No. 107A, formerly W. C. and E. R. No. 11 "Newton Manor," did a lot of work on the Northern Extension and nearly caused the demise of her driver, Tyson, and his mate when she burst her boiler at Seaton in 1880. Driver Tyson had No. 107A as his own engine for over 30 years. When the Furness began to work mineral trains over the Rowrah branch No. 107A and her sister, No. 109A, even penetrated onto the fragile tracks of the Rowrah and Kelton Fell (Mineral) Railway.

No. 109A was the regular engine of Driver Hugh McDowell, one of the most ardent Liberals in the township of Moor Row. It was only when these gallant old locomotives were approaching the half-century that they were released from their years of heavy pounding over the severe gradients of the C. and W. J. to earn respite on shunting duties in the Preston Street Goods Yard at Whitehaven. For a number of years 109A was frequently rostered to work a train of "beehive" coke from William Pit, Whitehaven, to Cleator Moor Ironworks. About 11-30 a.m. she would emerge from Whitehaven Tunnel at the Corkickle end, her arrival, with about a dozen or 15 coke wagons and brake, being announced by a "pop" on her deep-toned whistle.

Then there were the "Neddies": those first 0-6-0 side tanks supplied to the F.R. by Sharp, Stewart and Company for banking duties up both sides of Lindal Bank, between Ulverston and Barrow. When the larger 0-6-2 tanks came out at the beginning of the present century the "Neddies," still with their long side tanks, but mostly re-boilered by Mr. Pettigrew, gravitated to Moor Row.

It was not until 1898 that the Furness Railway produced any motive power specifically for the C. and W. J. and the "Joint Lines". In that year Mr. Pettigrew brought out three powerful 0-6-2 tanks, Nos. 112-14, with 18 by 26 inch cylinders. Built by Sharp, Stewart and Company, they were sent, when new, to Moor Row shed and worked mainly on the C. and W. J. throughout their life. This class was added to in 1912 and 1914, two more examples being added in each of these years. Numbered 92-95, they had larger boilers than their older sisters and were supplied by Kitson's, of Leeds.

Of tender types which ran over the system, these were usually a motley collection of 16 inch cylinder 0-6-0s – the famous "Sharpies" – in either their original or re-boilered form. Some were fitted with back-weatherboards for tender-first running, and, among the "regulars," were Nos. 49, 63, 66, 74 and 75. But on the whole, these engines did more duties on the "Joint Lines" than on the C. and W. J. A few of Mr. Pettigrew's 1898 class 0-6-0 goods engines also haunted the tracks from time to time, notably Nos. 7 and 8.

For handling the modest passenger train services on the system the Furness, at one time, provided one of their 2-4-0 tender engines, but later a couple of the 2-4-2 tanks rebuilds of the class were provided (usually Nos. 71 and 72). After the 1914-18 War, the 2-4-2 tanks gave way to a couple of Mr. Pettigrew's 1910 class 0-6-0 shunting tanks, plus, on occasions, one of his 4-4-2 tanks, usually confined to duties on the Coniston, Lakeside and Kendal branches.

In 1920 the following locomotives were more or less permanently allocated to the C. and W. J. R.:

Nos. 92-95, 112-14 (0-6-2 tanks), 10, 13 and 17 (1899 class 0-6-0s), 58, 60 (1910 class 0-6-0 tanks), 68/9, 82-4 ("Neddie" 0-6-0 tanks), 105/6A and 108-12A (ex. W. C. and E. 0-6-0 saddle tanks). A number of rebuilt "Sharpies" can be added to this list, but their composition varied from time to time. [2]

The engine sheds of the Cleator and Workington Junction Railway were at Workington, where all the Company's own locomotives were stabled, and at Siddick Junction. The latter, built to Furness design, housed four locomotives only. Moor Row shed, although it was just outside C. and W. J. territory supplied the majority of the engines doing duty over the line. [3]

Furness Railway 2-4-2 tank No. 70 stands at Siddick Junction awaiting its return journey with a passenger trains to Moor Row. This class of loco was rebuilt from the Sharp Stewart 2-4-0s which had been purchased for passenger working from 1870. Seven were rebuilt as 2-4-2Ts in 1891.

CRA Pattinson Collection
PA0348

Notes to Chapter Six

1.   Since the early 1950s, when Gradon was writing "The Track of the Ironmasters", some aspects of earlier C&WJR locomotive history have become a little clearer. Gradon admits to the doubtful history of *Rothersyke*, and it now appears probable that *Brigham Hill* and *Rothersyke* were one and the same engine.

Cleator and Workington Junction Railway Locomotive List

No.	Name	Type		Builder/no.		Date	Notes	Disposal
1	BRIGHAM HILL renamed in 1894 to							
	ROTHERSYKE	0-4-0(T)	OC	FJ	187	1882	New	(1)
2	ENNERDALE	0-4-0ST	OC	B	214	c1875	(a)	(2)
3	SOUTH LODGE	0-6-0ST	IC	RS	2553	1884	New	(3)
4	HARECROFT	0-6-0ST	IC	LE	196	1885	New	(4)
5	MORESBY HALL	0-6-0ST	IC	RS	2692	1890	New	(5)
6	BRIGHAM HILL	0-6-0ST	IC	RS	2813	1894	New	(6)
7	PONSONBY HALL	0-6-0ST	IC	RS	2846	1896	New	(7)
8	HUTTON HALL	0-6-0ST	IC	P	1134	1907	New	(8)
9	MILLGROVE	0-6-0ST	IC	P	1340	1919	New	(9)
10	SKIDDAW LODGE	0-6-0ST	IC	HC	1400	1920	New	(10)

Notes:

(a)   ex (Ward), Ross & Liddelow, contractors for Rowrah Branch, 12/1882.
(1)   Sold 3/1897; later to owners of West Stanley Colliery, Co.,Durham, and then to AB, c.1/1904.
(2)   to S.T.Croasdell, dealer, Workington, 7/1898 for £150.
(3)   to J.F.Wake Ltd., dealers, Darlington, Co. Durham, 7/1920.
(4)   withdrawn 9/1915, sold to Workington Iron & Steel Co. Ltd., No. 46.
(5)   withdrawn and scrapped 1919.
(6)   to LMSR 11564; withdrawn 11/12/1926 – and scrapped.
(7)   to LMSR 11565; withdrawn 18/12/1926 – and scrapped.
(8)   to LMSR 11566; withdrawn 3/12/1927 – and scrapped.
(9)   to LMSR 11567; withdrawn 5/12/1928 – and scrapped.
(10)   to LMSR 11568; withdrawn 22/6/1932 – to Hartley Main Collieries, Northumberland, via Robert Frazer & Sons Ltd., dealers, Hebburn, Co. Durham, 6/1932.

2.   Fuller details of these Furness Railway locomotives listed as working on the C&WJR during its last few years are as follows:

Type	FR No.	Builder/No.		Date	LMS No.	Withdrawn	Notes
Class 7 0-6-0 tender engines							
	10	NW	555	1899	12471	30/05/1930	
	13	SS	4563	1899	12474	14/08/1930	
	17	SS	4567	1899	12478	12/1929	
Class 55 0-6-0 tank engines							
	58	VF	2526	1910	11556	15/11/1932	(a)
	60	VF	2528	1910	11558	28/05/1935	(b)
Class 68 0-6-0 "Neddy Tanks"							
	68	SS	2204	1872	11549	04/1925	
	69	SS	2205	1872	11550	05/1925	
	82	SS	2300	1873	11551	10/1925	
	83	SS	2301	1873	11552	06/1925	
	84	SS	1843	1867	—	1918	(c)
Class 92 and 94 0-6-2 "Cleator Tanks"							
	92	K	5042	1914	11643	10/09/1934	(d)
	93	K	5043	1914	11644	01/09/1932	(d)
	94	K	4855	1912	11641	23/11/1934	(d)
	95	K	4856	1912	11642	09/1929	(d)
Class 112 0-6-2 Tank							
	112	SS	4364	1898	11622	12/1927	(d)
	113	SS	4365	1898	11623	3/1928	(d)
	114	SS	4366	1898	11624	4/1928	(d)

Ex-Whitehaven, Cleator & Egremont Railway 0-6-0ST

100A	FJ	21	1858	—	1918	(e)
105A	RS	1804	1867	—	1921	(f)
106A	RS	1798	1867	—	1918	(g)
107A	RS	1960	1869	—	1918	(h)
108A	AB	154	1875	11548	08/1924	(i)
109A	RS	1997	1871	11547	07/1924	(j)
110A	RS	2109	1873	—	1920	(k)
111A	RS	2110	1873	—	1920	(l)

The rebuilt "Sharpies" referred to by McGowan Gradon were various rebuilds of the 55 Class "29" 0-6-0s built by Sharp Stewart & Co. Ltd., of Manchester for the FR between 1866 and 1883. By 1920 the following rebuilt locomotives remained in service (LMS numbers and year of withdrawal in brackets; it is unlikely that locomotives withdrawn during before 1925 carried the allocated LMS numbers):

Class 29, rebuilt with Class 112 boiler from 1897:

25 (12002, 1924)	48 (12000, 1926)	61 (12001, 1925)
62 (12007, 1925)	66 (12003, 1925)	67 (12004, 1925)
71 (12014, 1925)	75 (12012, 1924)	76 (12006, 1925)
77 (12013, 1924)	78 (12005, 1925)	80 (12008, 1927)
85 (12009, 1925)	86 (12010, 1924)	87 (12011, 1924)

Class 29, rebuilt with Class 19 boiler from 1910 (locos marked * had large Pettigrew cab, others retained old Stirling-type cab):

49 (12075, 1928) *	50 (12076, 1927)	70 (12071, 1925)
72 (12072, 1927)	73 (12073, 1925)	74 (12074, 1925)
63 (12066, 1929) *	65 (12065, 1930) *	79 (12067, 1930) *
88 (12068, 1927)	89 (12069, 1927)	90 (12070, 1930) *

Notes:

(a) renumbered from FR No. 22 in 1918.

(b) renumbered from FR No. 24 in 1918.

(c) renumbered from FR No. 52 in 1915.

(d) ordered specifically for work on the C&WJR.

(e) formerly WC&ER No. 3 *Keekle*; became FR No. 100 in 1878, rebuilt by FR in 1882 and 1895; to duplicate list in 1904.

(f) formerly WC&ER No. 9 *Loweswater*; became FR No. 105 in 1878; rebuilt by FR (date not known); to duplicate list in 1904.

(g) formerly WC&ER No. 10 *Crummock*; became FR No. 106 in 1878; rebuilt by FR (date not known): to duplicate list in 1904.

(h) formerly WC&ER No. *Newton Manor*; became FR No. 107 in 1898; rebuilt by FR (date unknown); to duplicate list in 1904.

(i) formerly WC&ER No. 17 *Wastwater*; became FR No. 112 in 1878; rebuilt by FR in 1896 and 1915; renumbered FR No. 112 in 1898; to duplicate list in 1907.

(j) formerly WC&ER No. 13 *Springfield*; became FR No. 109; rebuilt by FR (date not known); to duplicate list in 1898.

(k) formerly WC&ER No. 14 *Derwentwater*; became FR No. 110 in 1878; rebuilt by FR (date not known); to duplicate list in 1907.

(l) formerly WC&ER No. 15 *Buttermere*; became FR No. 111 in 1878; rebuilt by FR (date not known); to duplicate list in 1907.

3. Siddick locomotive shed, at Dock Junction, was destroyed by fire on 23 February 1923. Its engines, staff and duties had probably already been transferred to the former LNWR shed at Workington. Workington Central C&WJR shed closed by May 1923 at the latest, again with locos, men and duties going to the former Workington LNWR shed.

Moor Row locomotive shed and works were built in the late 1850s to maintain and accommodate the locomotives and rolling stock of the Whitehaven, Cleator & Egremont Railway. After this company was taken over jointly by the LNW and Furness Railways in 1878 the shed and works came under the management of the latter company, and motive power for working Furness-operated services over the Joint Lines continued to be provided from Moor Row, all LNWR locomotives in West Cumberland being shedded at Workington. The agreement between the C&WJR and the FR for the latter to provide much of the motive power for the former, greatly strengthened the role of Moor Row shed which continued to provide motive power for the former LNWR & FR Joint and C&WJR lines until its closure on 31 July 1954. From this date all its locomotives, staff and duties were also transferred to Workington Motive Power Depot.

Under the LMS Moor Row became Western Division shed No. 39MR, then 12E from 1935, retaining this code until closure. Locomotives allocated to Moor Row on selected dates after 1923 were:

Furness Railway 0-6-2 tank No. 93 photographed in works grey livery by the builder, Kitson & Co., of Leeds in 1914. One of four similar locomotives built in 1912-14 for work on the C&WJR, they were known as the "Cleator Tanks".

CRA Collection

November 1928: ex-FR 2F 0-6-0s Nos. 12469, 12479, 12471; ex-FR 3F 0-6-2Ts Nos. 11627, 11635, 11636, 11637, 11638, 11639, 11640, 11641; ex-FR 2F 0-6-0Ts Nos. 11554, 11555, 11556; ex-L&YR 1F 0-6-2Ts Nos. 11619, 11621; Total: 16.

Summer 1934: ex-FR 3F 0-6-2T No. 11627; ex-L&YR 2F 0-6-0s Nos. 12025, 12027, 12063; ex-FR 2F 0-6-0 No. 12479; ex-FR 3F 0-6-0s Nos. 12494, 12497, 12499, 12510; ex-LNWR 0-6-0 No. 27609; Total: 10.

30 January 1954 (closure): ex-LMS 4F 0-6-0 No. 44461; ex-LMS 3F 0-6-0Ts Nos. 47337, 47390, 47525; ex-L&YR 3F 0-6-0s Nos. 52201, 52418; ex-FR 3F 0-6-0s Nos. 52494, 52499, 52501; Total: 9.

Abbreviations used in the notes above:

AB	Andrew Barclay, Sons & Co. Ltd., Kilmarnock.
B	Barclays & Co., Kilmarnock.
FJ	Fletcher, Jennings, Whitehaven.
HC	Hudswell, Clarke & Co. Ltd., Leeds.
K	Kitson & Co., Airedale Foundry, Leeds.
NW	Nasmyth, Wilson & Co. Ltd., Patricroft, Manchester.
P	Peckett & Sons Ltd.. Bristol.
RS	Robert Stephenson & Co. Ltd., Darlington.
SS	Sharp, Stewart & Co. Ltd., Atlas Works, Manchester.
VF	Vulcan Foundry Ltd., Newton-le-Willows, Lancashire.
OC	Outside cylinders.
IC	Inside cylinders.

Moor Row shed, from where the Furness Railway provided much of the motive power for work on the C&WJR. Two 0-6-0 tanks of very different vintages await duty: No. 57 on the left was built as No. 21 by Vulcan Foundry in 1910, and renumbered in 1918; No. 83 dated from 1873 and was built by Sharp, Stewart. At this time, about 1920, No. 83 would mainly have been employed in banking and local shunting work.

CRA Shillcock Collection SHI417

CHAPTER VII

THE TRAIN SERVICES

BECAUSE the main object of its existence was the transportation of minerals, the C. and W. J. R. never provided a lavish passenger service for its patrons. When the line was opened from Cleator Moor Junction to Workington in 1879 the following time-table was operated:

UP TRAINS

		a m	p m
MOOR ROW	dep.	9 20	1 45
Cleator Moor	„	9 25	1 50
Moresby Parks	„	9 32	1 57
Distington	„	9 40	2 05
High Harrington	„	9 43	2 08
WORKINGTON (Central) ...	arr.	9 50	2 15

DOWN TRAINS

		a m	p m
WORKINGTON (Central) ...	dep.	1030	4 00
High Harrington	„	1036	4 06
Distington	„	1041	4 11
Moresby Parks	„	1049	4 20
Cleator Moor	„	1055	4 26
MOOR ROW	arr.	1100	4 30

When the main line was extended to Siddick Junction the following increased service was put into operation from October 1880:

UP TRAINS

		a m	a m	p m
MOOR ROW	dep.	7 40	1012	2 45
Cleator Moor	„	7 45	1017	2 50
Moresby Parks	„	7 53	1025	2 58
Distington	„	8 01	1033	3 06
High Harrington	„	8 04	1036	3 09
Workington (Central)	„	8 11	1043	3 16
SIDDICK JUNCTION	arr.	8 15	1047	3 20

DOWN TRAINS

		a m	a m	p m
SIDDICK JUNCTION ...	dep.	8 25	1222	5 00
Workington (Central)	„	8 30	1227	5 05
High Harrington	„	8 35	1232	5 10
Distington	„	8 39	1236	5 14
Moresby Parks	„	8 47	1244	5 22
Cleator Moor	„	8 55	1252	5 35
MOOR ROW	arr.	9 00	1257	5 40

As the years went by the number of passenger trains was gradually increased until, in the final year of independent operation (1922), the following service was provided for its patrons by the "Track of the Ironmasters" :

UP TRAINS

		a m	a m	p m			S
MOOR ROW	dep.	7 20	9 50	1 15	4 50	6 20	——
Cleator Moor	„	7 24	9 54	1 19	4 54	6 24	——
Moresby Parks	„	7 31	10 01	1 26	5 01	6 31	——
Distington	„	7 39	10 09	1 34	5 09	6 38	7 30
High Harrington	„	7 43	10 12	1 38	5 15	6 42	7 35
Workington (Central)	„	7 50	10 20	1 45	5 22	6 50	7 40
SIDDICK JUNCTION	arr.	7 54	10 24	1 49	5 26	6 54	——

DOWN TRAINS

		a m	p m		S		
SIDDICK JUNCTION	dep.	8 05	12 05	5 35	——	8 20	——
Workington (Central)	„	8 15	12 12	5 42	7 00	8 45	——
High Harrington	„	8 20	12 17	5 47	7 05	8 50	——
Distington	„	8 24	12 21	5 51	7 10	8 55	——
Moresby Parks	„	8 32	12 29	5 59	——	9 02	——
Cleator Moor	„	8 39	12 36	6 06	——	9 10	——
MOOR ROW	arr.	8 43	12 40	6 10	——	9 14	——

S – Saturdays only

Note: the 8-20 p.m. from Siddick *arrived* at Workington at 8-25 p.m.

All services operated on week-days only. It will be noticed that the 1922 timetable was "unbalanced," there being an additional Up train. This was due to the provision of the 9-50 a.m. ex Moor Row, which gave a connection at Siddick Junction into the 10-10 a.m. "fast" train from Whitehaven to Carlisle. This M. and C. working stopped at Siddick at 10-36 and reached Carlisle at 11-45 a.m., giving connections to Scotland, the East and the South.

The "Track of the Ironmasters" also provided the following series of workmen's trains, in addition to the regular services just detailed. At 5-30 a.m. daily a train left Workington, reaching Moor Row at 6-04 a.m. It returned from Moor Row at 1-45 p.m. (one hour earlier on Saturdays), and arrived back at Workington at 2-17 p.m. (1-17 p.m. on Saturdays).

Another "workmen's" left Moor Row at 5-35 a.m. (5-10 a.m. on Saturdays) and ran to Moresby Junction, calling at Keekle Platform "halt" as well as Cleator Moor. The return working left Moresby Junction at 2-10 p.m. (1-10 p.m. on Saturdays). All these workmen's trains were run for the benefit of colliers living either in the Cleator Moor or Workington areas who worked at the Walkmill Pit of the Moresby Coal Company Limited. A small "halt" platform was provided at Moresby Junction, giving the miners a more convenient detraining point from which to reach the pit than at Moresby Parks station. The train from and to Workington also called at Moresby Junction "halt" in lieu of Moresby Parks. To-day Walkmill Colliery still draws coal, but the colliers reach the pit by bus, and the two "halt" platforms at Moresby Junction and Keekle have long been demolished. [1]

When the Northern Extension from Calva Junction to Linefoot was opened stations were built at Seaton and Great Broughton, although the line was constructed mainly for mineral traffic. Ultimately, the passenger service provided consisted of afternoon and evening trips to and from Workington on Wednesdays (Workington Market Day). A similar service was operated over the Rowrah branch to and from Arlecdon.

The passenger train service over the Lowca Light Railway is outlined in the chapter dealing with two mineral railways closely associated with the C. and W. J. R.   No passenger services were ever operated over the Moss Bay or Derwent Branches.

The goods and mineral services on the C. and W. J. were both extensive and complicated for so small a railway. This was perhaps inevitable on a main line which, in its modest 16 miles in length, boasted no less than nine junctions !

The complexity of the mineral traffic movements will perhaps be made clearer by listing the various blast furnaces, mines and quarries served by the railway, and also giving the general direction and nature of the traffic "flows" from the various concerns.

Starting from the Cleator Moor end of the line, the C. and W. J. had direct access to the blast furnaces of the Whitehaven Haematite Iron Company by a short branch which made a facing junction with the Down line at Cleator Moor station. It entered the ironworks' yard by an unprotected level crossing over the Whitehaven-Cleator Moor main road. All coke traffic into the plant went over this track. Iron ore, more conveniently, entered the works by a separate connection off the "Joint Line" at Birks Bridge Junction. By their connection, the Cleator and Workington Junction handled the bulk of the pig iron destined for Scottish steel makers produced by the Cleator Moor furnaces.

At Moresby Junction the Company tapped the whole output from Walkmill Colliery and the coke from the battery of ovens established there.

Passing on to Distington-Rowrah Branch Junction we find a heavy flow of additional traffic feeding into the main line. Iron ore from mines at Keltonhead and Knockmurton (on the R. and K. F. (M.) R.); limestone from Rowrah Hall and Salter quarries, and coal from Oatlands Pit. Hard by Distington station were the Distington Ironworks. Although the "Joint Line" got a share of the traffic to and from these furnaces the C. and W. J. got the main bulk, both inwards with coke and ore, and outwards with pig iron.

At Harrington Junction the Lowca, Moss Bay and Derwent Branches, giving access to Lowca Collieries and By-Product Plant and blast furnaces at Harrington, Moss Bay, and Derwent, brought more heavy loadings of coal and coke, iron ore, limestone, and pig iron. Beyond Workington (Central), Cloffocks Junction [2] gave connections into Oldside furnaces and the plant of the West Cumberland Iron Company, as well as access to Workington Dock for shipment coals. Up the Northern Extension line to Linefoot were collieries at Buckhill and Great Broughton. Finally, at Siddick, were sited the shafts of the St. Helen's Colliery and Brickworks Company.

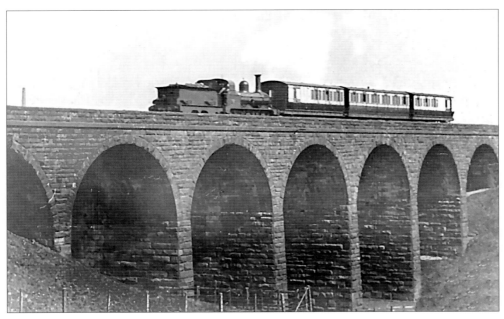

A Furness Railway "Sharpie" 0-6-0 crosses Keekle Viaduct with a train of FR carriage stock from Moor Row to Siddick Junction, probably in the 1890s. The chimney on the left is at Bowthorn Colliery.

CRA Shillcock Collection SHI435

It will be seen, therefore, that the "Track of the Ironmasters" ran like a main traffic artery through an area honey-combed with mines, quarries and ironworks. Surely, its "colours" should have been red, lined out in black and grey – the red of the rich Cumberland haematite, the black of the coal and coke, and the grey of the pig iron turned out from the many furnaces it served !

From the foregoing summary of the industrial concerns served by the C. and W. J. it will be appreciated that the freight schedule was a fairly complex one. To enumerate in detail all the workings as per the Working Timetable in force in October, 1919, would be very tedious, especially if the reader is not very well acquainted with the geography of the system. Perhaps a list of the various shed turns and principal through workings will give the clearest picture.

Starting at the northern end of the main line, Siddick shed sent out its No. 1 Duty at 5-0 a.m. This locomotive worked a workmen's passenger train from Workington to Lowca (over the Lowca Light Railway) and back. On return to Workington this engine then banked the 4-40 a.m. M. and C. Carlisle (Currock Yard) to Cleator Moor through freight from Workington up to Distington.

Siddick No. 2 Duty worked the 10-45 p.m. (except Saturdays) and the 7-10 p.m. (Saturdays only) through goods from Dock Junction to Carlisle (North-Eastern Yard). Except on Mondays, this engine returned from Carlisle with the 3-10 a.m. through mineral to Harrington Junction. Departure time on Saturdays was 10-30 p.m. from Carlisle. No. 3 Duty, off shed at 5-15 a.m., banked the return working of No. 2 Duty (except on Mondays) up to Harrington Junction. After giving this assistance it worked an empty mineral from Harrington Junction up the Northern Extension to Buckhill Colliery. Returning to Workington, this duty shunted the Central station yard until midday.

A trip from Siddick to Maryport and back to Harrington Junction, coming off shed at 8-45 a.m. and returning at 3-30 p.m., comprised No. 4 Duty.

Due out at 9-30 a.m., No. 5 Duty made a trip from Calva Junction over the Northern Extension to Linefoot Junction and back, coming on shed again at 4-25 p.m. Workmen's trains, except on Saturdays, and "market" trains on Saturdays, on the Lowca Light Railway, were handled by Nos. 6 and 7 Duties, the latter also putting in a goods trip (except on Saturdays) from Siddick to Distington Ironworks and back. These comprised the whole of the runs manned by Siddick shed.

Five turns ("A" to "E") were worked by the C. and W. J. locomotives stabled at Workington (Central) shed. These were made up of two duties over the Rowrah Branch; one separate turn over both the Derwent and Moss Bay Branches, and an additional trip over both branches by the same engine.

Moor Row shed manned "a baker's dozen" turns over the "Track of the Ironmasters," two of which finished out their time on the "Joint Line." The first turn (No. 10 Duty) was a curious one. It was known more usually as the "Circular Duty." It left Moor Row at 4-20 a.m. and worked an iron ore train to Moss Bay Works, via Whitehaven. Reaching Moss Bay at 5-45 a.m., it left again at 6-15 a.m. and worked up the Moss Bay Branch to Harrington Junction and so back to Moor Row at 7-30 a.m.

The first through trip over the main line, from Cleator Moor to Linefoot and return (No. 11 Duty) left the shed at 5-40 a.m. It was followed by No. 12 Duty (off shed at 5-30 a.m. SE and 5-5 a.m. SO) for passenger duties to Moresby Parks and Siddick. At 7-0 a.m. No. 9 Duty left for Distington Ironworks and No. 8 Duty, on passenger duties to Siddick and on the Lowca Light Railway, was out at 9-45 a.m. A trip to Workington Bridge and back (with coke traffic) occupied No. 15 Duty, which left the shed at 7-59 a.m. No. 14 Duty got away from Moor Row at 10-35 a.m., making a trip to Distington and up the Gilgarran branch as far as Wythemoor Colliery and return. A workmen's train to Workington followed by a goods trip to Siddick and back to Moor Row was No. 16 Duty, which left just after 4 p.m. and made a trip to Harrington Junction and Siddick. Moor Row shed supplied banking engine for both sides of the Moresby Parks "summit." No. 17 Duty ran as light engine to Harrington Junction each day at 6-30 a.m., from whence it operated until noon. No. 18 Duty did similar work from Cleator Moor Junction up to Moresby Parks. The two "C. and W. through goods" to Sellafield were worked by No. 19 Duty (from Harrington Junction in the mornings) and No. C13 duty (from Moresby Junction each afternoon).

41

Furness Railway 0-6-2T No. 98, seen here with a passenger train at Siddick Junction, was built by Nasmyth, Wilson & Co. of Manchester in 1904. This class would be seen on both goods and passenger workings on the C&WJR.

CRA Shillcock Collection SHI520

It will seen that the majority of the goods workings were short trips over certain portions of the line to serve the numerous mines, quarries and ironworks. Harrington Junction, which had quite a well-equipped and extensive marshalling yard, was the main focal point on which most of the traffic converged, and where it was re-marshalled for dispatch.

The following "through goods" were operated over the system.

At 4-40 a.m. a through working left the Maryport and Carlisle (Currock Yard, Carlisle) for Cleator Moor. During the 1914-18 War, in order to save locomotive power, an M. and C. engine and crew worked the train right through to Cleator Moor, where it terminated. The return trip left Cleator Moor at 9-0 a.m. and ran through to Maryport, to reach there at 11-5 a.m.

The through goods to and from the North-Eastern Yard at Carlisle, worked by Siddick shed, has already been mentioned. Southwards, off the system, there were two trips to Sellafield via Egremont. One, consisting of landsale coal from Walkmill Colliery, left Moresby Junction at 1-30 p.m., and the other, with southbound iron traffic from Moss Bay and Derwent Works, started from Harrington Junction at 5-30 p.m.

The return runs from Sellafield terminated at Moor Row in the late evening, traffic being worked forward to its various destinations the following morning.

The 8-50 a.m. mineral train from Siddick Junction to Maryport was also classed as a "through goods." As stated earlier in this chapter, this No. 4 Duty from Siddick shed returned from Maryport at 10-40 a.m. and ran through to Harrington Junction.

During the 1914-18 War, when traffic over the main line was at its heaviest, it was a regular practice to run two trains, coupled together and with a "banker" at the rear, up both sides of the Moresby Summit. For example, a train of coke for Cleator Moor Ironworks would leave Distington headed by one of the ex-W. C. and E. R. 0-6-0 saddle tanks (maybe 109A), behind this would be a rake of C. and W. J. 15-tonners, being worked empty to Walkmill Colliery and headed by a "Neddie." The whole double formation would be assisted in the rear by one of Mr. Pettigrew's 0-6-0 tanks.

From the Cleator Moor side, the writer remembers seeing a double formation labouring up past Keekle Platform in which four engines were involved. The train engine was a Furness "Cleator Class" 0-6-2 tank, hauling what the Americans call a "mixed consist" of freight. This was in turn banked by a 16-inch "Sharpie", which in turn was hauling a long train of coal empties, which was "tailed" by two bankers; a "Neddie" and an ex-W. C. and E. R. saddle tank.

After April 1st, 1918, the practice of coupling two mineral trains together with a "banker" in rear was prohibited after dark; although the method continued to be used during daylight. Later, the general falling off of traffic put an end to it altogether.

A Control Office (known as the "Regulator's Office") was operated at Harrington Junction. It was open each week-day from 5-30 a.m. to 9-30 p.m.

Although the "Track of the Ironmasters" possessed no passenger coaches it did own nearly 250 wagons. These were of 10 and 15 tons capacity. The former mostly had wooden "dumb" buffers. The 15-tonners were high-sided and used mainly for the "washed small" traffic from Walkmill Colliery. They were painted red, with "C. and W." in large, white letters on the sides.

Between Cleator Moor Junction and Siddick, Tyers 1 wire, 2-position semaphore instruments were used. They were also in use on the Northern Extension line and the Rowrah Branch. Just before the 1923 amalgamation, 3-position type instruments were put in between Cleator Moor and Siddick. On the Lowca Light Railway, Tyer's No. 5 Tablet instruments were employed, which the Moss Bay and Derwent Branches were worked by Staff and Ticket. Phonophore type telephones were used on the C. and W. J. R. and the signal frames were Tyer's tappet-locking type.

On account of the number of severe gradients on the "Track of the Ironmasters" loading restrictions were severe. On the main line, Class A locomotives (F. R. 0-6-2 tanks and the 1899 Class 0-6-0s) were restricted to 250 tons on gradients of 1 in 70 and to 150 tons on the Rowrah Branch. The older 0-6-0 tanks were limited to 190 and 100 tons on the same lines, and the "Sharpies" a mere 160 and 75 tons respectively. The length of any train on the main line was limited to 65 empty wagons for the most powerful locomotives and 45 on the Rowrah Branch. On the falling gradient down to Workington from Harrington Junction, all mineral trains were halted at Calva Junction for brakes to be unpinned and for examination. Catch Points were provided on the Up main line south of both Moresby Parks and Moresby Junction, on the 1 in 70 gradient, and on the Down line north of Distington station (also on a 1 in 70 gradient), and on the 1 in 95 gradient north of High Harrington.

Notes on Chapter Seven

1. Walkmill Colliery continued to draw coal until February 1961 and its closure was a major factor in precipitating the closure of much of the C&WJ line from September 1963 (see Appendix A).

2. The original text seems to miss a line here. Cloffocks Junction provided a connection with the Cockermouth and Workington line of the LNWR, over which coke from County Durham, which had travelled via Stainmore Summit and Keswick, came onto the C&WJR to supply the ironworks on the line. Dock Junction (just south of Siddick) provided connections into the Oldside and Lowther Ironworks, and to Workington Dock.

CHAPTER VIII

INDUSTRIAL LOCOMOTIVES

BECAUSE the "Track of the Ironmasters" served so many large industrial concerns within its territory, and also because I realise that there are a considerable number of railway enthusiasts to whom the purely industrial locomotive particularly appeals, I have included this short chapter in the story of the C. and W. J. R. For much information I am indebted to my friend, Mr. Bernard Roberts, of the Industrial Locomotive Society. [1]

Starting at the Cleator Moor end of the system, the Whitehaven Haematite Iron Company operated a number of locomotives in the furnace's yard. Originally, the furnaces of the concern were located at Lonsdale Ironworks, close to Bransty Station, Whitehaven, but these were closed at the turn of the last century. [2] There, it is understood, five four-wheeled saddle tanks, all built by Andrew Barclay, of Kilmarnock, and with cylinders varying in diameter from 10 to 14 inches, were employed. It is not known whether any of these engines were transferred to Cleator Moor. Apparently none of this first batch of locomotives bore names.

At the Cleator Moor Ironworks the following locomotives are known to have been used:

"Aldby" : A Fletcher, Jennings "patent" four-wheeled well tank, with 12 by 20 inch cylinders. Built in 1867 and Works Number 66. Date of scrapping unknown.

"Millgrove": A 14 by 18 inch cylinder saddle tank supplied new by the Lowca Engineering Company (successors to Fletcher, Jennings) in 1889. Works Number 203. Disposal unknown.

Originally, W. C. and E. R. 0-4-0 saddle tank "Ullswater," this locomotive was obtained from the L. and N. W. R. at Crewe during the 1914-19 War. She was built by Barclay in 1875, and was scrapped in 1919. Another four-wheeled saddle tank, unnamed, was obtained from the Parkside Mining Company, Frizington. Built by Barclays and Company (an off-shoot of the main Barclay firm) and rebuilt by the Lowca Engineering Company in 1890, she had cylinders of 10 by 18 inches.

Andrew Barclay supplied "Stonecross" in 1908 and "Moresby Hall" in 1909. Both were saddle tanks with 14 by 22 inch cylinders. After the Cleator Moor Ironworks were acquired by the Millom and Askam Haematite Iron Company these two engines, on the shutting down of the Cleator Moor furnaces, were transferred to Millom, were they still work. [3]

The New Lowca Engineering Company, in 1912, supplied "Croft End" (0-4-0ST) to Cleator Moor. In 1933 she was sent to the Florence Iron mine, of the Millom Iron Company, at Egremont. Another four-wheeler, "Almeida," was rebuilt at Lowca in 1920. Both her origin and ultimate disposal are uncertain. At one time Cleator Moor Ironworks are believed to have employed two other engines, named "Hollins" and "Linethwaite," as well as a Neilson-built 0-4-0 saddle tank with 12 by 18 inch cylinders.

The Walkmill Pit of the former Moresby Coal Company started off with three of Fletcher, Jennings' "Improved Patent" four-wheelers. The first, with 10 by 22 inch cylinders, was delivered in 1879. The next two, with cylinders 12 by 22, were delivered in 1881 and 1885.

The next one delivered in 1885 was the last engine to be built at Lowca by Fletcher, Jennings: the firm thereafter becoming the Lowca Engineering Company. In due course, this little band of "Lowcaites" were scrapped and were replaced by the present-day stud of three Andrew Barclay products. All are four-wheeled saddle tanks, and were built as follows: No. 1 (13 by 20 inch cylinders) in 1898; No. 2 (12 by 20 inch) in 1903; and No. 4 (14 by 22 inch) in 1911. At Oatlands Pit, on "Baird's Line," there worked one of Lowca Engineering Company's "Class A" saddle tanks with 14 by 20 inch cylinders. Known at "No. Two," she was sent to Workington Dock when Oatlands Pit shut down, and is still working there. [4]

The Lowca Engineering Company at Parton built many locomotives for work in the coal and iron industries of West Cumberland. This "Class A" 0-4-0ST for Charles Cammell's Derwent Works at Workington was built in 1899 and worked until 1947.

Peter W Robinson Collection

Peckett 0-4-0 tank "Bristowe Hill" was supplied new to the Harrington Ironworks by Peckett & Sons of Bristol in 1911. After the works closed it worked at Moss Bay and then Harrington Colliery until it was scrapped in 1962. Bristowe Hill was the home of C&WJR director Sir John Randles M.P. who was also chairman of the Workington Iron & Steel Company.

Peter W Robinson Collection

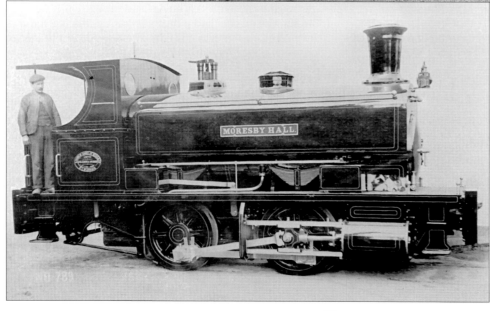

"Moresby Hall", an 0-4-0ST built by Andrew Barclay, Sons & Co. of Kilmarnock, worked at the Cleator Moor Ironworks of the Whitehaven Hematite Iron & Steel Co. from delivery new in 1909. It was named after the home of Sir James Bain M.P.

CRA Kerr Collection KER301

The first locomotive recorded as working at the Distington Ironworks was an Andrew Barclay product of standard industrial pattern built in 1880, Works No. 204. In 1890 another engine was supplied by the same builders (Works No. 659). In company with the earlier engine, the latter went to the Prince of Wales Dock, Workington, for shunting duties. Known as "Distington No. 4," she is now No. 14 in the United Steel Company's list. The latter firm, of course, absorbed the Workington Iron and Steel Company, which had in turn taken over the Distington plant. "Distington Brand" pig iron is still made at Workington to this day, although it is 25 years since the Distington plant went out of blast. The last engine went to Distington in 1920. Built by Kerr, Stuart and Company, she is now No. 57 on the U. S. C list. [5]

On the Northern Extension Line, at Buckhill Colliery, the Allerdale Coal Company (whose pit, Buckhill was) employed a Lowca-built "Class A" saddle tank with 14 by 20 inch cylinders. [6]

Notes on Chapter Eight

1.   McGowan Gradon was very selective in the industrial concerns which he chose to include in this chapter. It includes only those establishments directly connected in later days with the C&WJR main line, plus one each on the Northern Extension and the Rowrah branch. He could also have included several further iron and steel works, collieries, brickworks and quarries, all of which were served by the C&WJR. In updating Gradon's information, most of which was pretty accurate, to take account of researches over the last 50 years, the original coverage has more or less been maintained, otherwise this publication would have to include details of a large proportion of the industrial locomotives of West Cumberland - not an appropriate task for this book.

The following industries were connected at some time to the C&WJR but are not included in the detailed notes below. Locations marked * probably had their own locomotives at some time.

Cleator Moor	Bowthorn Colliery (closed in 1894)
	Crowgarth Iron Ore Mines, (from 1882 to closure in September 1930)
Harrington:	Harrington Harbour (closed early 1920s)
Harrington	Ironworks (closed early 1920s) *
High Harrington	Barf's Quarry,
	Glebe Sand Siding
	Hall Green Sand and Gravel Siding
Rowrah	Rowrah Hall Quarry (closed 1978) *
Seaton	Camerton Brick Works and Colliery
Workington	Brokenshaw's Dock Siding
	Derwent Iron & Steel Works *
	Lonsdale Dock *
	Lowther Iron Works *
	Moss Bay Iron & Steel Works *
	Oldside Iron Works *
	St. Helen's No. 3 Colliery (closed 1966) *
	Siddick Sand Siding
	Westfield Wagon Works (closed by 1962) *
	Workington Storage Co. *

2.   There was no connection between the ironworks at Cleator Moor and those at Whitehaven Bransty. The Lonsdale Hematite Iron Co. was formed in 1870 by Messrs. Barclay, Craig & Co. of Kilmarnock and built four blast furnaces on the Bransty site. After repeated financial difficulties the company was twice reformed, finally going into liquidation in 1902. The Cleator Moor works had a much longer life, the first furnace being erected there in 1841 by Thomas Ainsworth. After formation of the Whitehaven Hematite Iron Co., three furnaces were operated. Gradon's confusion may have arisen from the take-over of this company in 1920 by the North Lonsdale Iron Co. Ltd. of Ulverston. The works finally closed in 1927.

3.   Locomotives known to have worked at the Cleator Moor Ironworks (all standard gauge) are -

Name/number	Type	Cyls	Builder	No.	Date	Origin	Disposal
—	0-4-0ST	OC	N	571	1860	New	(c)
ALDBY	0-4-0T	OC	FJ	66	1867	New	Scrapped
LINETHWAITE	0-4-0ST	OC	N	1558	1870	New	(d)
HOLLINS No. 2	0-4-0ST	OC	AB	120	1872	New	Scr. c.1912
MILLGROVE	0-4-0ST	OC	LE	203	1889	New	Scr. 1909
STONE CROSS	0-4-0ST	OC	AB	1126	1908	New	(e)
MORESBY HALL	0-4-0ST	OC	AB	1166	1909	New	Scrapped
CROFT END	0-4-0ST	OC	NLE	250	1912	New	(f)
ULLSWATER	0-4-0ST	OC	AB	138	1873	(a)	Scr. c.1919
ALMEIDA	0-4-0ST	OC	AB	114	1871	(b)	(g)

Notes:
(a)   Purchased from Ackers, Whitley & Co., Leigh, c.1914; was earlier WC&ER No. 16 ULLSWATER.
(b)   Purchased from Parkside Mining Co., Frizington.
(c)   Sold in 1862 to the Whitehaven & Furness Junction Railway as No, 15, later FR No. 50 named either BOB RIDLEY or PHOENIX, and sold in 1883.
(d)   May have been sold to Solway Hematite Iron Co., Maryport by 1873.
(e)   To Millom & Askam Hematite Iron Co. Ltd., Millom, c. 1936.
(f)   To Millom & Askam Hematite Iron Co. Ltd., Florence Mine, Egremont, c.1933.
(g)   Possibly to Millom & Askam Hematite Iron Co. Ltd., Millom, c. 1920.

4.   The Moresby Coal Co. was formed in 1879 to sink a large colliery at Walkmill near Moresby Parks station, connected to the C&WJR main line by a short branch from Moresby Junction. A further mine was also started at Oatlands, west of Distington, but was not rail-connected until completion of the Rowrah Branch in 1882. The village of Pica was built nearby to provide accommodation for miners. A bank of coke ovens was erected at Walkmill in 1911, but closed in 1936 upon the opening of new coke ovens at Workington Iron & Steel Works, the Moresby Coal Co. having been acquired by the United Steel Companies in 1924. Oatlands closed in November 1930, but Walkmill worked through into the period of nationalisation from 1947, and was eventually closed in February 1961.

Locomotives of the Moresby Coal Co. Ltd., all standard gauge, were -

At Walkmill Colliery, Moresby

Name/number	Type	Cyls	Builder	No.	Date	Origin	Disposal
MORESBY No. 1	0-4-0T	OC	FJ	162	1879	New	Scrapped
MORESBY No. 2	0-4-0T	OC	FJ	179	1881	New	Scrapped
MORESBY No. 3	0-4-0T	OC	FJ	192	1885	New	Scrapped
MORESBY No. 1	0-4-0ST	OC	AB	824	1896	New	(a)
MORESBY No. 3 (originally MORESBY No, 4)							
	0-4-0ST	OC	AB	1189	1911	New	(a)
MORESBY No. 2	0-4-0ST	OC	AB	981	1903	(b)	(a)

At Oatlands Colliery, Pica

Name/number	Type	Cyls	Builder	No.	Date	Origin	Disposal
OATLANDS No. 1	0-4-0ST	OC	AB	981	1903	New	(b)
No. 2	0-4-0ST	OC	LE	244	1906	New	(c)

Notes:
(a)   Passed to National Coal Board at nationalisation on 1 January 1947.
(b)   Acquired new by the company as OATLANDS No. 1, transferred to Walkmill on closure of Oatlands. Fitted with vacuum brakes for working the Oatlands-Arlecdon miners' trains.
(c)   To Workington Dock on closure of Oatlands.

5.   The Distington Ironworks was established in 1878 and was originally rail served by the Gilgarran branch of the Whitehaven, Cleator & Egremont Railway, though later much traffic was handled by the C&WJR via Distington Junction. The company was never part of the original "Combine" of the Workington Iron & Steel Co. Ltd., formed in 1909, which in turn amalgamated with the United Steel Companies in May 1919. From this date the Distington Hematite Iron Company Ltd. also became part of the USC. However, the works only operated sporadically during the 1920s and were abandoned, and demolished after 1929.

The locomotives which worked at Distington Ironworks, all standard gauge, were:

Name/number	Type	Cyls	Builder	No.	Date	Origin	Disposal
No. 1	0-4-0ST	OC	AB	204	1880	New	(a)
—	0-4-0ST	OC	A.Barr		no details known		Scrapped
ROSENEATH	0-4-0ST	OC	LE	197	c. 1887	New	Scrapped
DISTINGTON No. 4	0-4-0ST	OC	AB	669	1890	New	Scrapped
SCOTIA	0-4-0ST	OC	AB	659	1880	(b)	(a)
DISTINGTON No. 5	0-4-0ST	OC	KS	4179	1920	New	(a)

Notes:
(a)   To Workington Iron & Steel Works on closure of Distington, c. 1929.
(b)   From James Sparrow & Sons, Ffrwd Ironworks, North Wales, c.1904.

During World War 2 much of the Ironworks site was redeveloped for a new factory providing high quality castings and forgings for the aircraft industry. High Duty Alloys Ltd. also had a rail connection onto the former Gilgarran branch with their own locomotive until 1954, after which the declining traffic was shunted by British Railways locomotives working the local pick-up goods. One loco worked on this site, "H.D.A. No. 1", built by Andrew Barclay; it was an outside cylinder 0-4-0ST (No. 2169 of 1943) and supplied new. As traffic declined it was sold in 1954 to Glynhir Tinplate Co. Ltd. at Pontardulais in West Glamorgan, and BR locos shunted the site when necessary.

6.   The Allerdale Coal Co. Ltd owned a number of collieries in West Cumberland, two of which were on the Northern Extension of the C&WJR. Buckhill Colliery had been sunk in 1873 by the West Cumberland Iron Co. which worked it until 1887. After a short period of ownership by Messrs. Fletcher & Waugh it was taken over by the Allerdale Company in 1888. Its original rail connection had been via a branch from the Cockermouth & Workington line of the LNWR, but this closed when the Northern Extension was opened in 1887. Thirty beehive coke ovens were erected at Buckhill in 1890, but went out of use about 1910 from when coal was sent to William Pit at Great Clifton for coking. The colliery ceased to wind coal in November 1932 and the site later became part of

the Royal Naval Ammunition Depot which had an extensive internal narrow-gauge rail system.

Only one locomotive is known to have worked at Buckhill Colliery. This was "ALLERDALE No.1", an outside cylinder 0-4-0ST supplied new by Lowca Engineering (No. 211 of 1891).

Alice Colliery was located close to the junction with the Maryport & Carlisle Railway at Linefoot. It was sunk in 1898 by Messrs. Wilson & Williamson and passed to the Flimby & Broughton Moor Coal & Firebrick Co. Ltd. in 1906. The pit closed in 1921. No locomotives which worked there have been specifically identified.

ABBREVIATIONS USED:

OC   Outside cylinders
AB   Andrew Barclay, Sons & Co. Ltd. Kilmarnock
A.Barr Andrews, Barr & Co., Kilmarnock
FJ   Fletcher, Jennings, Lowca, Whitehaven
KS   Kerr, Stuart & Co. Ltd., Stoke-on-Trent
LE   Lowca Engineering Co. Ltd., Lowca, Whitehaven (successors to Fletcher,   Jennings)
N   Neilsen & Co. Glasgow
NLE   New Lowca Engineering Co. Ltd., Lowca, Whitehaven (successors to Lowca Engineering)

A steel sided iron ore wagon of 20 tons capacity was owned and operated by the Distington Ironworks. Built by Charles Roberts of Wakefield, it was fitted with a hoppered bottom for ease of unloading.
CRA Collection

CHAPTER IX

THE END OF THE RUN

THE last meeting of the Cleator and Workington Junction Railway was held at Workington on February 8th, 1923. In their last report the Directors stated that the gross receipts during 1922 had totalled £91,267 12s 4d, and, after deducting Debenture Interest, &c., there remained a credit balance of £21,220 11s 0d. This was distributed as follows: Interim and final dividend on Preference Shares, £10,420 1s 0d; Interim dividend of 2 per cent. and final dividend of 3 per cent. absorbing £10,800 10s 0d.

The Board of Directors at the Amalgamation comprised the following gentlemen, the majority of whom were Ironmasters: Sir John S. Ainsworth, D.L., Harecroft, Gosforth, Cumberland (chairman); William Little, Hutton Hall, Penrith (deputy chairman); Joseph Ellis, Skiddaw Lodge, Keswick; Sir John S. Randles, Bristowe Hill, Keswick; Thomas Ainsworth, The Flosh, Cleator, Cumberland; Sir Frederick J. Jones, Irnham Hall, Grantham, Lincolnshire; Albert O. Peech, Firbeck Hall, Rotherham; and James V. Ellis, Calva House, Workington.

At the time of its absorption into the London, Midland and Scottish Railway, the "Track of the Ironmasters" comprised 12 miles and 12 chains of double track (of which 10 miles 79 chains was the main line from Cleator Moor to Siddick) and 12 miles 70 chains of single line. The minor and mineral branches added a further 6 miles and 37 chains of single and 1 mile and 7 chains of double track. Including all sidings the grand total of trackage was 61 miles and 44 chains.

Six 0-6-0 saddle tanks were on the books in 1923. Rolling stock comprised 194 wagons up to 12 tons and 30 up to 20 tons. There were also six locomotive coal wagons and five brake vans.

During 1922 the C. and W. J. locomotives ran a total mileage of 32,517 miles. Of this total nearly 200 miles was on banking duties. During the same year the Furness locomotives ran over 150,000 miles on the system, of which barely a third was on passenger duties and over 5,000 miles on banking work. On the passenger side, only 198 first-class fares were issued, but third-class totalled 111,449 fares, and workmen's no less than 364,388. These earned a total income of £6,570 12s 8d. Only seven season tickets were taken out during the year, and only one was a first!

The preponderance of goods and mineral traffic is shown by the fact that during 1922 the amount carried was 811,872 tons, which earned £84,349 4s 2d. Of the total tonnage, coal and coke accounted for 488,757 tons; pig iron 100,847 tons, and limestone 94.415 tons. Out of the total tonnage carried, 687,495 tons originated on the C. and W. J. system.

For working their "lion's share" of the traffic on the "Track of the Ironmasters" the Furness Railway was paid £15,793 12s 3d by the C. and W. J. R.

The Company owned four horses and carts for good delivery and nine cottages.

The last meeting of shareholders was held at Workington on February 28th 1923. At this meeting, it was announced that £72 was to be paid for each £100 of C. and W. J. R. stock "Less than we hoped for," remarked the Chairman, "but the United Steel Company, who hold 95 per cent. of the Ordinary shares, are satisfied, and, if they were, then the ordinary shareholders should also be."

It was agreed, on the motion of Mr. James Cameron, that four years' fees (£2,000) should be voted to the Directors for loss of office; this was agreed by the meeting.

The deputy chairman, Mr. William Little, regretted the absence of Sir John Ainsworth. The latter, who was the only remaining original member of the Board, had held the position for 47 years. Mr. R. E. Highton, who proposed a vote of thanks to the Chairman, proved himself to be (in the author's opinion) a remarkably accurate prophet when he said: "I regard the passing of the railway, and those who have been working so actively for the good of the district, with mixed feelings. I am not certain that it is to the advantage of the community at all. As a matter of fact, I think it will be a disadvantage."

A vote of thanks to all the officials of the Company included a special reference to the secretary and general manager, Mr J. A. Haynes, whose services were not being retained by the L. M. and S. R.

The following evening a farewell dinner was given by Mr. J. A. Haynes at the Central Hotel, Workington. Some 150 people were present and, in the course of a survey of the history of the "Track of the Ironmasters," Mr. Haynes paid tribute to the long services of many of the staff, a list of whom is given below:

All with over 35 years' service: John Bell, guard; John Ray, stationmaster; Tom Smith, ganger; Jacob Younghusband, goods agent; Tom Sanderson, storekeeper; John Hodgson, guard; John Norman, permanent way inspector; John McLean and William Campbell, stationmasters; Robert Edgar, mason; Joseph Poole and Charles Nicholson, engine drivers.

Mr. Haynes said they still had seven pensioners on their books, with services ranging from 25 to 40 years.

The peak traffic year, said Mr. Haynes, was 1909, when their little railway handled 1,644,514 tons of freight.

During the 1914-18 War, 37 of their staff served in the forces, six losing their lives.

Mr. Haynes, Mr. Hugh Murray (engineer) and Mr. Wood (accountant) were later presented with suitable mementoes of the occasion by I. Ray, who proposed the toast of the officials. Various items, including two specially composed for the occasion, which are reproduced on pages 54 and 55, were given during the course of the evening.

Mr. Haynes, who was not retained by the L. M. and S. R., emigrated to Australia. The following "thumb-nail" sketch appeared in the *West Cumberland News* of February 24th, 1923: "A real railwayman. Rushed through life like an express. Sticks to the main line. As obliging as a guard; as obliging as a porter. As curt as a booking clerk, as firm as a ticket collector. As industrious as a stoker, as grim as a driver, as adept as a coupler."

With the cessation of the Durham coke traffic to the Distington and Cleator Moor furnaces via the C. K. and P. R. and the Workington Bridge-Cloffocks Junction spur, the latter was taken up. At the same time, the Northern Extension was cut back from Linefoot to Buckhill.

When Buckhill Colliery closed down the remainder of the Northern Extension might have suffered a similar fate had not the Admiralty established a munition dump near Broughton Moor a year or two prior to 1939.

The Workington Dock Branch was removed in January, 1937, and, in 1939, it was decided to work the limestone traffic from Rowrah Hall Quarries to Moss Bay and Derwent blast furnaces of the United Steel Companies via Marron Junction and the Cockermouth-Workington section. In that year, therefore, except for about half-a-mile of track from Rowrah towards Arlecdon, the whole of "Baird's Line" was lifted.

Track maintenance on the C. and W. J. section deteriorated after the withdrawal of the passenger services in 1931. To-day, the line is mainly ash ballasted, and a considerable portion is concrete sleepered. Although many of the original C. and W. J. signals have been replaced by upper quadrants, quite a number of the old ones remain. The Moss Bay Branch is still *in situ*, but is not used. The Derwent Branch continues to be utilised by the U. S. Companies' trains from Lowca Colliery. [1]

Probably the reason why the main line has not been singled is because it serves as a "stand-by" route between Workington and Whitehaven. Landslides onto the track between Parton and Harrington, where the line runs close to the sea and below steep cliffs, as well as the never-ending repairs to Whitehaven tunnel, have proved the value of the "Track of the Ironmasters" in emergencies. For several years, in order to facilitate repair work in Whitehaven tunnel at week-ends, the morning Down Sunday mail from Carnforth to Whitehaven terminated at Corkickle, from whence passengers for north of the town were conveyed to Bransty station by bus. The "Class 5" or "Jubilee" which usually works this turn, then proceeded light, and tender first, up Corkickle Bank to Moor Row and over the C. and W.J.R. to Siddick, and so back to Workington (Main) and the shed. The locomotive returned to Corkickle in like manner in the afternoon to work the Up mail to Carnforth at 6 o'clock.

Another present day working of the line was instituted following the establishment of a depot of the Milk Marketing Board at Egremont. Every day, Sundays included, a milk train for Newcastle-on-Tyne leaves Egremont at 4 p.m., and after reversal at Moor Row, travels over the C. and W. J. to Siddick. The other regular scheduled trips are a goods, working from Moor Row to Siddick and back, and one from Siddick to Moresby Junction and return. The latter, a Workington shed turn, deals with the coal output from Walkmill Colliery, the washed small from which now goes to the Central Coking Plant of the U. S. C. at Workington for treatment. The only new industry sited on the line is at Distington, where High Duty Alloys, of Slough, built a big factory during the Second World War, mainly on the old ironworks site. To-day, this factory only works to partial capacity, but a certain amount of traffic is lifted daily by the Moor Row working.

After withdrawal from service of the C. and W. J. and more elderly types of Furness engines from the area, the declining traffic was handled mainly by the small band of ex-Furness locomotives remaining at Moor Row shed.

To work limestone traffic over the Rowrah Branch during the last few years of operation the L. M. S. used a couple of their "standard 3F" 0-6-0 shunting tanks. Three of the engines are shedded at Moor Row to-day, and one of them works the Moor Row-Siddick freight.

The author made a footplate trip over the "Track of the Ironmasters" early in 1949. Our steed was ex-F. R. 12499 (as she was then), and that noted Moor Row character, Jack Fisher, was driving. We ran light to Egremont to collect "the milk"; two L. M. S. bogie vans, plus an ex-N. E. R. six-wheeler. After the return to Moor Row and "run-round," away we went, tender first, at 5-5 p.m. for Siddick.

12499, in common with the majority of "rolling ruins" which make up the stud at Moor Row shed, was in poor shape. Her major ailment was the tendency of her reversing lever, when running backwards, to jump into forward gear. In order to prevent his steed from indulging in this prank as she strained at the collar up the 1 in 70 gradient from Cleator Moor to Moresby Junction, Jack Fisher had hung a full bucket of coal onto the end of the lever. In the gathering dusk we panted through Moresby Parks and then, as we hit the 1 in 70 down towards Distington, Jack "let her go." Round several curves of 25 chains radius, and less, we rocketed, the keen night air making my eyes water. Past the overgrown remains of the Rowrah Branch, easing a bit round the long curve into Distington station, then down past Harrington Junction, past silent and deserted signal boxes, and with no signal lamps lit, until we reached Calva Junction. Here the box was open on account of a freight working up to Broughton Moor Dump. Arriving at Siddick, we put our train away in the loop, ready for collection by one of Ivatt's ugly 2-6-0s from Workington shed, which would work the train on to Carlisle. The trip had all the qualities of a run over a "ghost" railway; a railway haunted by the spirits of West Cumberland's industrial past, and, most of all, by the spirits of those local industrialists whose sturdy independence brought about the construction, 75 years ago, of the "Track of the Ironmasters."

Notes to Chapter Nine

1.   Gradon appears to have got these references to the Derwent and Moss Bay branches reversed. It is understood that the Derwent Branch link over the Whitehaven Junction line, into the former Derwent Works, closed in the 1930s, though it remained in use as far as Wilkinson's Wagon Works until 1962. The Moss Bay branch was the route used by USC trains to Lowca until its final closure in 1973.

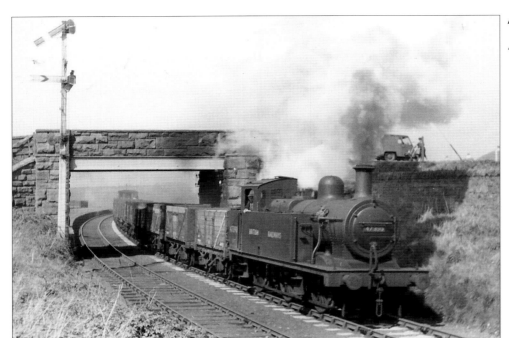

Heading a train of coal empties south through High Harrington is ex-LMS Class 3F 0-6-0T No. 47390 on 7 May 1954.

F W Shuttleworth

Leaving Workington Central in the evening sunlight on 15 March 1952 is ex-LMS Class 4F 0-6-0 No. 44461 with a returning football excursion to Moor Row and Egremont.

CRA Dendy Collection DEN162

Ex-Furness Railway 0-6-0 No. 52509 and crew pose for the photographer at Moor Row station as they wait to proceed with a very mixed collection of hopper wagons on 7 May 1954.

F W Shuttleworth

At Harrington Junction two United Steel Co. 0-4-0 diesels head down the Moss Bay branch with a heavy train from Lowca.

M J Andrews

Menu cover for the farewell dinner for held for C&WJR staff held at the Central Hotel, Workington on 29th February 1923.

CRA Collection

The Secretary and General Manager's

FAREWELL DINNER

At the Central Hotel, Workington, on Wednesday, 28th February 1923

RECITATION by ADAM HOLMES, Signalman

This night will be long remembered
　　By the Staff of the Cleator Line,
While sitting around the table;
　　It's all very grand and fine.

But when we think of how we're met
　　With one we are going to part
I think we all assembled here
　　Will feel it in our heart.

To lose a friend that has been kind
　　In far more ways than one,
There's others in the outside world
　　Will miss him when he's gone.

The town in general (poorer still)
　　I mean in financial gains;
In all good causes you would find
　　The name of Mr Haynes.

When anything out of the ordinary
　　He looked to his master's gains,
So the Public, too, will miss him
　　In providing special trains.

It seemed he always looked ahead
　　His aim and purpose to defend,
In trying e'er what he could do
　　To raise more dividend.

In all the years that have gone past
　　Since he took up the reins
We never hear a wrongful word,
　　But good – of Mr. Haynes.

The C. and W. has lost its name
　　Of course we have no objection;
Today we're known by another name
　　The C. and W. Section.

This Grouping System which has come,
　　Great change it has wrought;
For this is one of Geddes' plans
　　He engineered and fought.

Other changes – sure to come –
　　We cannot stay their hand,
They say it's for the country's good
　　And benefit all the Land.

We cannot let this night go by
　　without our thanks to mention,
The good things we've received tonight
　　It passes comprehension.

Please do accept our grateful thanks
　　It's every heart's desire,
And many years may you be spared;
　　From Work you now retire.

Then, when settled in your home,
　　From care and worry free,
May Health and Happiness bless your life
　　In the land across the sea.

Then let us stand before we part
　　With heart and hand combine,
And sing with voice the grand old tune
　　In the days of Auld Lang Syne.

The Secretary and General Manager's

FAREWELL DINNER

At the Central Hotel, Workington, on Wednesday, 28th February 1923

SONG: "THE CLEATOR AND WORKINGTON"
Composed by J. Holmes, Stationmaster

(To the tune of "John Peel")

We are met here tonight, just to have a jolly time,
We are all lads alike, that work on the Cleator Line;
And the lads on the line are the boys that can shine,
When they turn out to work in the morning.

There's the Stationmaster here, they call him Tommy Leach,
He's as active as a hare, and as sweet as any peach,
His stature is so small, and he has so far to reach,
When he turns out to work in the morning.

D'ye ken the X Rays, Number One and Number Two?
The eyes of these Johnnies, they really pierce you through,
They make things hum of the C. and W.,
When they turn out to work in the morning.

D'ye ken Billy Campbell, the Railway Man so bluff,
He's really a polished gem, although he is so rough,
He can drink a pint of ale, or sample any stuff,
When he goes out to work in the morning.

D'ye ken John McLean? He married late in life;
He must have been afraid he'd be bitten by a wife,
But he has got a duck to comfort him through life,
And he needn't go to work in the morning.

Yes, we ken Jack Dixon, and Gainford Joe,
The two lads who fear neither friend or foe;
The row of these two when they are on the go
Would waken up the dead in the morning.

D'ye ken Billy Reed, with his old black bag?
He tortured us with rules and how to use a flag;
But he'll trouble us no more, 'mid the mountains and the crag,
For he's off to retire in the morning.

While we sing of the lads who still carry on,
On the different Railways knocked into one,
Let us honour the memory of those that are gone,
And toil not with us in the morning.

D'ye ken Mr Haynes, the gentleman so true?
His friends they are many, his foes they are few;
His friends will miss him when he goes on the blue
To join his sons abroad in the morning.

We wish him god speed, both he and his wife,
And health and great joy in his new sphere of life,
Three cheers for Mr. Haynes, who has spent most of his life
On the Railway down here every morning.

EPILOGUE

Although the Cleator and Workington Junction Railway ceased to exist as a separate entity in 1923 portions of it still remain in use today. A brief survey of the line's career, first as a small section of the London, Midland and Scottish Railway, and today, as a still smaller segment of British Railways, will round off the story of the "Track of the Ironmaster." Owing to the changed face of industry in West Cumberland, it is a sad story for the railway enthusiast.

With the steady onset of the depression which smote West Cumberland in the late 1920s the traffic on the Cleator and Workington Junction section of the L. M. and S. R. steadily declined. By 1930, both the Cleator Moor and Distington Ironworks were idle, iron ore mines, from which traffic was worked by the section, were either worked out or flooded, and Oatlands Colliery was almost worked out. On the Northern Extension line, Buckhill Colliery was a similar case. Practically the only sources of mineral traffic served by the C. and W. J. section alone were the limestone quarries at Rowrah and Walkmill Colliery, at Moresby Parks.

Motor bus competition caused the withdrawal of the passenger services between Moor Row and Siddick Junction on April 13th, 1931.

So wrote William McGowan Gradon in 1952. At that time there still remained the main line, plus the Harrington and Moss Bay branches, part of the Derwent branch, and the Northern Extension as far as Broughton Moor. Local goods stations remained open at Seaton, Workington, High Harrington, Distington and Moresby Parks. Quantities of traffic were still being generated by the Ammunition Depot at Broughton Moor, from High Duty Alloys at Distington and from Walkmill Colliery; and the United Steel Company's trains continued to link Workington Iron and Steel Works with the company's subsidiary plants on the Lowca Light Railway and Harrington Colliery. The main line of the Cleator & Workington, from time to time, also provided a significant diversionary route when the coastal line between Workington and Whitehaven was closed for maintenance works, during attacks by the sea from below, or from falling cliffs from above. Since then all has disappeared, leaving no remnant of the Cleator & Workington Junction Railway in operation.

As McGowan Gradon indicated in his brief epilogue, the Great Depression of the late 1920s and early 1930s dealt a very severe blow to the industries which the railway served. In all truth, serious decline had already set in some years earlier as many of the iron mines in the Cleator District closed as their reserves became either exhausted or too expensive to work in competition with cheap imported ores. After the General Strike in 1926 very few remained at work, with the exception of the newer mines south of Egremont. Some had been maintained on a "care and maintenance basis", but were eventually abandoned and became flooded.

Still independent until 1920, when it was taken over by the North Lonsdale Iron Co., of Ulverston, the Cleator Moor ironworks survived until October 1927: it took another twelve years until its demolition. The site is now occupied by an industrial estate, all trace of its furnaces, buildings, slag tips and railway lines having disappeared long ago. The works put much of its production out onto the Cleator & Workington line, but when dependency on foreign ores became essential, it was hopelessly sited in competition with Workington. Distington Ironworks went the same way. Taken over by the United Steel Companies in 1919, it closed as early as 1922. The loss of both these works made serious inroads into the traffic of the railway which served them.

Coal mining along the C&WJR was to carry on for some years after Gradon was writing, though most pits on the line had closed long before. In 1923 there remained collieries at Buckhill on the Northern Extension, worked by the Allerdale Coal Co. (closed in 1932). At Siddick Junction stood St. Helen's No. 3 Colliery. Coke ovens here provided coke for local iron and steel works, and the colliery itself was taken over by the Untied Steel Cos. in 1943, but was to be closed by the National Coal Board in July 1966. However, the major coal mine which sustained the line up to its final decline was the Walkmill Colliery of the Moresby Coal Co. This was also taken into the United Steel Companies' fold in 1924, nationalised in 1947 and was to continue working under the National Coal Board until closure in February 1961. This event brought an inevitable end to much of the Cleator & Workington main line, that part from Moor Row to Distington Junction closing from 16 September 1963, when the section from Harrington Junction to Distington was reduced to a single line siding. Any remaining through traffic was diverted through Whitehaven. The loss of traffic at Distington led in turn, on 26 September 1965, to the cutting back of the line to Calva Junction. The section from Siddick was singled at the same time, but retained for access to Broughton Moor via the remaining part of the Northern Extension.

Through varying fortunes and managements the Royal Naval Ammunition Depot, Broughton Moor was to survive throughout the "Cold War" period, becoming a casualty of a new era of east-west international relations, with its final closure in December 1992. The last known revenue-earning train, removing munitions from the site, ran on 4 June 1992 and the little-known narrow and standard gauge railways which connected the various parts of the site were torn up and sold off.

Of the branches, we have already read of the closure of that to Rowrah in 1938. The Workington Dock branch had already closed in 1936, and the next to go was the Derwent Branch from Harrington Junction. When built this had directly served the works of the Derwent Hematite Iron Co., which were taken over and much enlarged by Charles Cammell & Co. Ltd., when they moved their production facilities from Dronfield in Derbyshire to Workington in 1882. Part of the Workington Iron & Steel Co. from its formation in 1909, the works were integrated with the adjacent Moss Bay plant in the 1930s and use of the Derwent branch declined, especially after the diversion of the Rowrah limestone traffic via Marron Junction.

Long disused, it was finally closed in 1952, leaving only that part which connected with the works of Wilkinson's Wagons Ltd. The works, and the branch which connected it to Harrington Junction, survived until 1962. Closure of the final two C&WJR branches, to Moss Bay and Harrington came on 23 May 1973. A direct connection between the two branches at Harrington Junction – and their disconnection from the main line – was implemented after the closure of the main line, and the whole route to Lowca was leased by British Railways to the United Steel Co. For more information see note 4 to Chapter 5.

Today the most conspicuous reminder of the Cleator & Workington Junction Railway and the drive and enterprise behind its creation is the seven-arch viaduct at Keekle, near Cleator Moor, with its fine background of the Lake District fells. Sometimes, in the stillness of a cold, clear day, one can almost imagine the stirring sights and sounds of a heavy train of iron ore, starting off in the distance from Cleator Moor Junction, train engine and banker getting to grips with their train as the gradient steepens to 1 in 70, then plodding steadily towards Moresby Summit under vast plumes of smoke and steam.

Perhaps the industries the railway linked could be harsh and uninspiring, but all in various ways combined to create and support an industrial community which has now largely disappeared.

Last days at Broughton Moor – a BR Class 31 diesel heads along a very overgrown Northern Extension near Camerton with a load of narrow gauge track parts in 1989.

Peter Robinson

APPENDIX A

CHRONOLOGY OF THE
CLEATOR & WORKINGTON JUNCTION RAILWAY

The following chronology aims to list the principal dates in the history of the Cleator & Workington Junction Railway, from its first inception to the closure of the final section. A wide variety of official and non-official sources have been searched for this information which does not claim any degree of completeness. Dates for opening and closing of stations are given in Appendix G.

Royal Assent to Act of Parliament authorising the C&WJR main line from Cleator Moor to Siddick Junction, plus branches to Lonsdale Dock, Harrington and Derwent. 27 June 1876

Royal Assent to Act of Parliament authorising working of the CWJR by the Furness Railway (working agreement of 6 April 1877 scheduled to the Act). 28 June 1877

Royal Assent to Act of Parliament authorising branch from Distington to Rowrah (Baird's Line). 4 July 1878

Agreement with Moresby Coal Co. for provision of junction and sidings at Moresby Junction. 30 May 1879

Opening of main line, Moor Row Junction to Siddick Junction, plus branches from Harrington Junction to Derwent Iron Works and Harrington Rosehill, and connections to Lowther Ironworks and St.Helen's Colliery, for mineral traffic. 1 July 1879

Royal Assent to Act of Parliament authorising the Furness Railway Company to hold up to £25,000 shares in the CWJR. 21 July 1879

Opening for general goods traffic. 4 August 1879

Opening of main line, Moor Row to Workington, for passenger traffic. 1 October 1879

Opening of connection to Whitehaven Hematite Iron & Steel Co.'s works at Cleator Moor. August 1880

Opening of main line, Workington Central to Siddick Junction, for passenger traffic. 1 September 1880

Royal Assent to Act of Parliament authorising branch from Distington Joint station to Distington Iron Works (powers later abandoned). 3 July 1881

Opening of Rowrah Branch, Distington Rowrah Branch Junction to Rowrah Junction, to mineral traffic. 1 May 1882

Opening of connection to Workington Iron Works. August 1882

Opening of Rowrah Branch, Distington to Arlecdon, to passenger traffic. 3 July 1883

Royal Assent to Act of Parliament authorising the Northern Extension from Calva Junction to Brayton Junction (M&CR and Solway Junction Rly.), also
    (1) Cloffocks curve from Cloffocks Junction to Workington Bridge (LNWR),
    (2) Moss Bay/Harrington Ironworks branch from Harrington Junction. 16 July 1883

Opening of Parkside Siding, Rowrah. August 1883

Opening of Cloffocks-Workington Bridge curve. March 1885

Opening of Moss Bay branch. 19 December 1885

Royal Assent to Act of Parliament authorising abandonment of that part of the Northern Extension beyond Linefoot, and the creation of a junction at that point with the Maryport & Carlisle Railway. 25 June 1886

Opening of Northern Extension, Calva Junction to Linefoot Junction, to mineral traffic. 24 March 1887

Opening of Buckhill Colliery connection. 24 March 1887

Opening of Northern Extension from Calva Junction to Seaton for passenger traffic. 4 January 1888

Running powers Distington Joint-Distington Iron Works ended. 31 July 1888

Opening of connection at Dixon's Quarry, Rowrah. June 1889

Opening of connection to Camerton Colliery. February 1890

Opening of connection to Oatlands stone quarry.	February 1890
Opening of Harrington Harbour branch.	7 July 1893
Opening of Outfields Colliery connection near Linefoot.	November 1895
Running powers Distington Joint-Distington Iron Works re-commenced.	9 March 1896
Completion of new offices at Workington Central station.	March 1897
Opening of engine shed and wagon shops at Workington Central.	November 1897
Second class passenger accommodation abolished.	1 January 1898
Agreement with Postmaster General to carry mail bag daily between Workington and Distington and Workington and Siddick daily, except Sundays, Christmas Day and Good Friday for £12 per annum.	January 1898
Opening of Alice Pit (Linefoot) connection.	May 1898
Opening of connection to St. Helen's Coke Ovens.	May 1908
New signal cabins erected at Seaton and Oatlands.	1909
Agreement with Workington Iron & Steel Co. Ltd. for latter to work own traffic over C&WJR between Derwent Works and Rosehill Junction, via Harrington Junction.	7 June 1911
Light Railway Order approved to allow use of Harrington & Lowca line by passenger traffic.	16 May 1913
Harrington Junction-Lowca opened for passenger traffic.	2 June 1913
Traffic Control cabin erected at Harrington Junction.	1919
New signal cabin erected at Moresby Parks.	1919
Closure of line: Buckhill Colliery-Linefoot Junction.	22 August 1921 (official date: 1 September 1921)
Cleator & Workington Junction Railway merged into London Midland & Scottish Railway.	1 January 1923
Closure of locomotive sheds at Workington Central and Dock Junction.	1923
Withdrawal of passenger service: Harrington Junction-Lowca.	31 May 1926
Closure of line: Moss Bay-Harrington Harbour	Fell into disuse from 1928
Closure of line: Wilkinson Wagon Works-Derwent Works (part of Derwent Branch).	1930s
Closure of line: Cloffocks Junction-Workington Bridge (curve removed).	26 March 1930
Withdrawal of passenger services: Moor Row to Siddick Junction.	13 April 1931
Closure of line: Dock Junction-Workington Dock.	27 July 1936
Closure of line: Distington Rowrah Branch Junction-Rowrah Junction.	8 August 1938
Remaining parts of C&WJR system became part of British Railways, London Midland Region.	1 January 1948
Connection removed: Rose Hill Junction, connection to Harrington Harbour.	May 1952
Connection removed: Barf's Quarry siding.	April 1953
Closure of locomotive shed at Moor Row.	31 July 1954
Closure of line: Wilkinson Wagon Works-Harrington Junction (last part of Derwent Branch).	1962
Closure of line: Moor Row No. 2-Distington Joint (exclusive); track singled Distington Joint- Harrington Junction; closure of signal boxes at Moresby Junction, Moresby Parks and Distington Joint (reduced to ground frame status, taken out of use from 1 June 1964).	16 September 1963
Closure of token cabin at Rosehill Junction.	15 June 1964
Closure of line: Calva Junction-Distington Joint (exclusive); track singled Calva Junction-Siddick Junction; closure of signal boxes at Calva Junction, Workington Central and Harrington Junction.	26 September 1965
Closure of line: Moss Bay-Harrington Junction-Rosehill-Lowca.	23 May 1973
Closure of line: Siddick Junction-Calva Junction-RNAD Broughton Moor (day after last revenue earning train).	4 June 1992

RAIL TOURS OVER THE CLEATOR & WORKINGTON

During the 1950s and 60s a number of rail tours provided opportunities for railway enthusiasts to traverse remaining sections of the Cleator and Workington line. Only the first of these was able to travel over the full length of the main line, from Siddick to Cleator Moor Junction. Running on 6 September 1954, it was organised jointly by the Manchester and Stephenson Locomotive Societies and covered many remaining obscure lines in West Cumberland. Starting from Sellafield, it was hauled by former Furness Railway 0-6-0 No. 52501 (Furness Railway No. 20), first to Moor Row, where it reversed to travel over the metals of the northern arm of the former Whitehaven, Cleator & Egremont Railway to Marron Junction, thence to Workington Main where sister locomotive No. 52499 (FR No. 28) was attached in the rear to draw the train back to Siddick Junction. The two locos together then worked the train to Calva Junction where another reversal took the train up the remaining section of the Northern Extension to the gates of the Ammunition Depot at Broughton Moor – probably the only time that main line coaching stock ever travelled over this line. The train then returned, running through Calva Junction to Workington Central. Here was another halt to detach 52499 from the rear, leaving 52501 to work the train up the remaining stretch of 1 in 70 to Harrington Junction and onwards over Moresby Summit to Moor Row to complete the trip over the C&WJR. The tour terminated at Whitehaven Bransty: it was to be the only railtour to visit to the C&WJR in main line coaching stock.

It was to be twelve years before another tour ventured on to Cleator & Workington metals, this time in brake-vans. On 7 May 1966 "The Solway Ranger", sponsored by the Railway Enthusiasts' Club of Farnborough, started from Workington Main, hauled by Class 4MT 2-6-0 No. 43006, and made its way via Siddick and Calva to Buckhill. The train then had to re-trace its route, the locomotive propelling as necessary, as the main line south of Calva had disappeared by this time.

Only one more tour was to repeat this procedure. The Stephenson and Manchester Locomotive Societies enjoyed a further West Cumberland brake-van tour on 2 March 1968, this time starting from Carlisle and hauled by Clayton Type 1 Bo-Bo No. 8510. Travelling south after their Buckhill trip, they were to leave former LNWR metals at Moss Bay and travel over the Moss Bay branch of the C&WJR to Harrington Junction, thence via Rosehill and the Lowca Light Railway, regaining the main line at Parton, via Harrington No. 10 Colliery and Bain's Siding on the stub of the former Gilgarran branch of the Whitehaven, Cleator & Egremont Railway. This routeing, without the Buckhill visit, was repeated on 26 May the following year by the Border Railway Society's brake-van special, "The Furnessman". This time the two United Steel Company 0-4-0 diesels were met at Rosehill by National Coal Board 0-6-0ST *Amazon* which provided

banking assistance over Copperas Hill and through to Harrington No. 10 Colliery at Lowca. The 0-6-0 saddle tank then took the train solo to No. 4 Pit Siding on the former WC&ER Parton branch where BR haulage resumed.

This was not new territory for the Border Railway Society. The Carlisle-based group had first persuaded the United Steel Company to run an evening outing, in two of the company's own brake-vans, from Moss Bay to Lowca in June 1967, and this was to be repeated at least once before 26 May 1973 when a farewell trip – and last train – was run for them over the line.

The only other known rail tour to venture onto Cleator & Workington metals was at the east end of the Rowrah Branch, where a stub of the branch had been left since 1938 as a headshunt for reaching Rowrah Hall Quarry. While several tours visited Rowrah, only one, it is believed, travelled up this short line from Rowrah Junction, this being on 15 March 1969, when again the MLS/SLS visited West Cumberland. This time they were travelling in a pair of Cravens-built Class 113 diesel multiple units which was easily able to work back from Rowrah Junction to the buffer stops just short of the former station at Arlecdon.

An unidentified railway worker posing in front of the nameboard at Siddick Junction station CRA Pattinson Collection PA0665

The first railtour to visit the C&WJR was the "West Cumberland Rail Tour" organised jointly by the Manchester and Stephenson Locomotive Societies on 6 September 1954 seen here standing at Distington station behind ex-Furness Railway 0-6-0 No. 52501.

CRA Dendy Collection DEN005

Calva Junction with "The Solway Ranger" railtour run by the Railway Enthusiasts' Club of Farnborough on 7 May 1966. Ex-LMS Class 4MT 2-6-0 No. 43006 starts to run round the train of brakevans prior to propelling them up the Northern Extension to Buckhill.

CRA Collection M00755

"The Solway Ranger" at Buckhill on 7 May 1966.

CRA Collection M00759

DISTANCE TABLES & TRACK DIAGRAMS

Main Line and Northern Extension

Miles chains

0 00	Cleator Moor Junction (start of C&WJR, junction with LNWR & FR Joint Lines)
0 25	Cleator Moor
	Keekle Colliers' Platform
2 48	Moresby Junction
3 12	Moresby Parks
6 31	Distington Station (junction with LNWR & FR Joint Lines)
6 78	Barf's Quarry Siding
7 42	High Harrington
8 10	Harrington Junction
9 52	Workington (Central)
9 67	Cloffocks Junction
10 17	Workington Bridge
10 17	Calva Junction
	11 71 Seaton
	14 26 Buckhill
	15 21 Great Broughton
	16 09 Alice Pit
	16 47 Linefoot Junction (M&CR)
10 66	Dock Junction
	11 79 Workington Dock
11 26	Siddick Junction (LNWR)

Track lifting at Copperas Hill in August 1973.

Peter Robinson

Rowrah Branch

0 00	Distington Rowrah Branch Junction
2 38	Oatlands
6 03	Arlecdon
6 37	Rowrah Junction

Harrington Branch and Lowca Light Railway

0 00	Harrington Junction (C&WJR)
	Harrington Church Road
	Archer Street
1 35	Rosehill Junction (C&WJR/LLR)
0 00	do.
	Copperas Hill
1 54	Micklam
2 04	Lowca

LONDON & NORTH
WESTERN
AND CLEATOR &
WORKINGTON RAILWAYS
NOTICE.
THIS FOOTBRIDGE IS THE PRIVATE
PROPERTY OF THE RAILWAY
COMPANIES, AND IS PROVIDED
FOR THE USE OF PASSENGERS
TO AND FROM THE STATION.
BY ORDER

Cast iron notice displayed on the footbridge at Siddick station.
CRA Pattinson Collection PA0664

Distance tables for the other branches are not available.

62

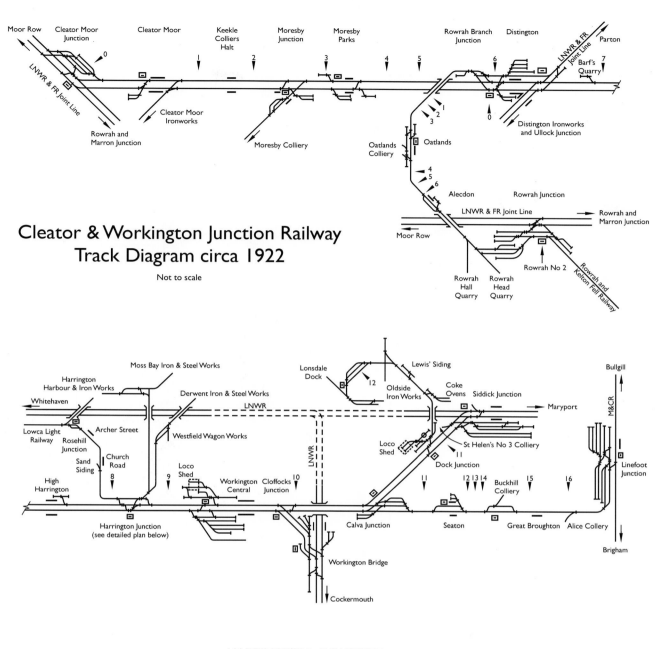

Cleator & Workington Junction Railway
Track Diagram circa 1922
Not to scale

Moor Row

Cleator Moor Junction

Cleator Moor

Keekle Colliers Halt

Moresby Junction

Moresby Parks

Rowrah Branch Junction

Distington

LNWR & FR Joint Line

Parton

Barf's Quarry

LNWR & FR Joint Line

Rowrah and Marron Junction

Cleator Moor Ironworks

Moresby Colliery

Oatlands Colliery

Oatlands

Distington Ironworks and Ullock Junction

Alecdon

Rowrah Junction

LNWR & FR Joint Line

Rowrah and Marron Junction

Moor Row

Rowrah No 2

Rowrah and Kelton Fell Railway

Rowrah Hall Quarry

Rowrah Head Quarry

Moss Bay Iron & Steel Works

Harrington Harbour & Iron Works

Derwent Iron & Steel Works

Lonsdale Dock

Lewis' Siding

Bullgill

Oldside Iron Works

Coke Ovens

Siddick Junction

Whitehaven

LNWR

Maryport

M&CR

Lowca Light Railway

Rosehill Junction

Archer Street

Westfield Wagon Works

Loco Shed

St Helen's No 3 Colliery

Linefoot Junction

Sand Siding

Church Road

Loco Shed

Dock Junction

High Harrington

Workington Central

Cloffocks Junction

LNWR

Buckhill Colliery

Harrington Junction
(see detailed plan below)

Calva Junction

Seaton

Great Broughton

Alice Colliery

Brigham

Workington Bridge

Cockermouth

HARRINGTON JUNCTION

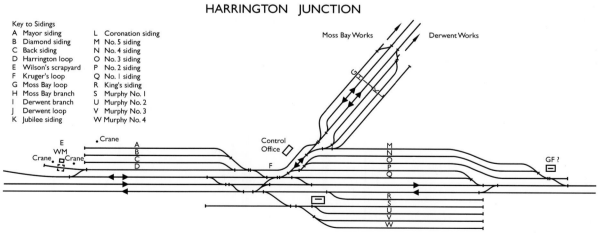

Key to Sidings
A Mayor siding
B Diamond siding
C Back siding
D Harrington loop
E Wilson's scrapyard
F Kruger's loop
G Moss Bay loop
H Moss Bay branch
I Derwent branch
J Derwent loop
K Jubilee siding

L Coronation siding
M No. 5 siding
N No. 4 siding
O No. 3 siding
P No. 2 siding
Q No. 1 siding
R King's siding
S Murphy No. 1
U Murphy No. 2
V Murphy No. 3
W Murphy No. 4

Moss Bay Works

Derwent Works

Crane

Control Office

GF ?

Based on LMS line diagrams, Barrow District Engineer's Office plans (Cumbria Record Office TBR2 series) and Ordnance Survey 1:2500 plans (1925 edition)

APPENDIX D

GRADIENT DIAGRAMS

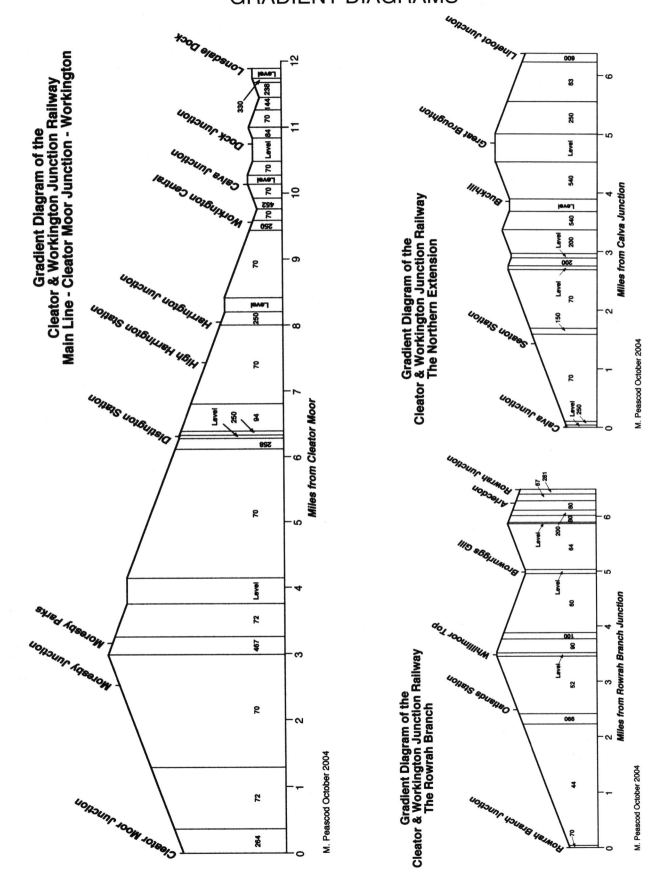

APPENDIX E

DIRECTORS OF THE
CLEATOR & WORKINGTON JUNCTION RAILWAY

All persons who served as directors of the company are listed below. Some enjoyed many years in office, whereas others, the 3rd Earl of Lonsdale, for instance, only a few months. Where possible information has been presented on other principal interests and commitments of the individuals concerned during their lifetime. Though this is far from complete it does show how many of the early directors of the Cleator & Workington Junction Railway were closely involved in the iron and steel industry, especially in West Cumberland. Some also had strong Scottish connections, and later in the company's life, when most of the company's shares were held by the United Steel Company, directors were appointed to represent that interest.

David AINSWORTH D.L., J.P.
  (b. 2 March 1842, d, 21 March 1906, brother of Sir John, q.v.)
Director: 1900 – 1906
Residences:
  The Flosh, Cleator; Wray Castle, Windermere
Other directorships:
  Maryport & Carlisle Railway Co. 1874 – 1906
    (Deputy Chairman 1904-1906)
  Lindal Mining Co.
  Economic Fire Office
  The Whitehaven News Ltd.
M.P. (Liberal)
  for West Cumberland 1880 – 85,
  for Egremont 1892 – 1895

Sir John Stirling AINSWORTH Bt., D.L., J.P., L.L.B., M.P.
  (b. 30 January 1844, d. 24 May 1923)
  Created baronet 1917
Director: 1876 – 1923
  Deputy Chairman: 1893 – 1900
  Chairman: 1900 – 1923
Residences:
  The Flosh, Cleator; Harecroft, Gosforth;
  Arndanaiseig, Loch Awe, Argyllshire;
  55 Eaton Place, London SW
Proprietor: Ainsworth & Co. (Cleator Moor iron mines)
M.P.
  for Argyllshire 1903 – 1918
  (Unsuccessfully stood for Barrow 1886)
Lt.Col. commanding 3rd Volunteer Battalion, Border Regt.
  1898 – 1902
High Sheriff of Cumberland: 1891

Thomas AINSWORTH B.A. (Cantab.)
  (b..8 February 1886, d. ??) 2nd baronet from 1923
Director: 1916-1923
Residences:
  The Flosh, Cleator; Harecroft, Gosforth

James Robert BAIN D.L., J.P., F.R.G.S., M.P.
  (b. 1851, d. 28 February 1913)
Director: 1876 – 1905
Residences:
  Ellerbank, Harrington; Moresby Hall, Whitehaven;
  Bolton Hall, Gosforth; 7 Sloane Court, Chelsea
Other directorships:
  Cumberland Union Bank
  Chairman of the Cumberland Coal Owners
    Association
M.P. (Conservative)
  for Egremont 1900 – 1906
Colonel: 3rd Battalion Border Regiment (Cumberland
  Militia)

Jonas Lindow BURNS-LINDOW
  (b. 29 April 1849, d. 30 March 1893)
Director: 1880 – 1882
Residences:
  Ehen Hall, Cleator; Irton Hall
Other directorships:
  Whitehaven, Cleator & Egremont Railway (1871 – 1877)
Iron Ore mining proprietor
High Sheriff of Cumberland 1877

William BURNYEAT D.L., J.P.
  (b. 8 November 1849, d. 28 June 1921)
Director: 1900 –1921
Residence:
  Millgrove, Moresby
Shipowner and Iron Merchant (Burnyeat, Dalzell & Co.)
Other directorships:
  Furness Railway 1906 – 1920
    Deputy Chairman 1917 – 1920
  Moss Bay Hematite Iron & Steel Co.
  Workington Iron & Steel Co.
  The Whitehaven News Ltd.

Edward CARLISLE
  (b. c.1880, d. ??)
Director: 1905 –1908
Residences:
  Buck Grove, Workington; Ashfield, Workington

Henry Frazer CURWEN J.P., D.L.
  (b. 18 April 1834, d. 6 March 1900)
Director: 1876 – 1880
  Deputy Chairman July – August 1876
  Chairman: August 1876 – 1880
Residences:
  Workington Hall; Belle Isle, Windermere
Landowner and colliery lessor
High Sheriff of Cumberland, 1888

Thomas Steele DODGSON
  (b. 17 May 1823, d. 8 January 1891)
Director: 1885 – 1891
Previous employment
  Traffic Manager, L & C R, Carlisle (?? – 1863)
  Secretary & General Manager, Whitehaven, Cleator
  & Egremont Railway (1863 – 1877)
  Secretary & General Manager, C&WJR (1878 – 1885)

James Valentine ELLIS
Director: 1921 – 1923
Residence:
  Calva House, Workington
Other directorships:
  Workington Iron & Steel Co.

Joseph ELLIS
Director: 1902 – 1923
Residences:
    Skiddaw Lodge, Keswick;
    Cheetham Hill, Manchester
Other directorships:
    Moss Bay Iron & Steel Co.
    Workington Hematite Iron Co.
    Workington Iron & Steel Co.

William FLETCHER D.L., J.P., F.G.S., M.P.
    (b. 31 January 1831, d. 6 August 1900)
Director: 1876 –1900
    Deputy Chairman: 1876 – 1880
    Chairman: 1880 – 1900
Residence:
    Brigham Hill, Cockermouth
Other directorships:
    Cockermouth & Workington Railway (1863 – 1866)
    Allerdale Coal Co.
    Moresby Coal Co.
    West Cumberland Iron & Steel Co.
M.P. for Cockermouth 1879 – 80
Chairman of Cumberland County Council 1889 – 1892

George Geddes GLEN J.P.
Director: 1908 – 1917
Residences:
    Grecian Villas, Harrington: Ellerbank House, Harrington
Other directorships:
    Harrington Iron & Coal Co. Ltd. (to 1909)
    Workington Iron & Steel Co. (1909 – ??)
Chairman: Harrington Urban District Council

Major Andrew GREEN THOMPSON J.P.
    (b. 1820, d. 27 April 1889)
Director: 1876 – 1889
Residences:
    The Hollies, Keswick; Bridekirk
Other directorships:
    Cockermouth, Keswick & Penrith Railway (1863 – 1882)
    Maryport & Carlisle Railway (1877 – 1888)
MP for Cockermouth (April – November 1868)

Robert Ernest HIGHTON J.P.
    (b. 1858, d.??)
Director: 1906 – 1909
Residences:
    Newlands, Workington; Threlkeld Leys, Cockermouth
Other directorships:
    Cockermouth, Keswick & Penrith Railway (1914 – 1923)
    Moss Bay Hematite Iron & Steel Co. Ltd. (General
        Manager)
    Distington Hematite Iron Co.
    Workington Iron & Steel Co. (from 1909)
Member: Cumberland County Council
Mayor of Workington 1902 – 1905, 1910 – 1914
Hon. Major, 1st Cumberland Royal Garrison Artillery
    (volunteers)

Robert JEFFERSON D.L., J.P.
    (b. 1826, d. 1902)
Director: 1880 – 1901
Residence:
    Rothersyke, Egremont
Wine and Spirit merchant
Other directorship:
    The Whitehaven News Ltd.

Sir Frederick John JONES Bt., J.P.
    (b. 1854, d.??) Created Baronet 1919
Director: 1919 – 1923

Residence:
    Irnham Hall, Grantham, Lincolnshire
Other directorships:
    Workington Iron & Steel Co.
    United Steel Cos.
    British Wagon Co.
President: Mining Association of Great Britain
President: South Yorkshire Coal Trade Association
President: Coal Conciliation Board for England & Wales

William. LITTLE J.P.
    (b. c.1833. d. ??)
Director: 1893 – 1923,
    Deputy Chairman 1904 – 1923
Residence:
    Hutton Hall, Penrith
Solicitor and Agent to the 4th Earl of Lonsdale

Henry LOWTHER, 3rd Earl of Lonsdale
    (b. 27 March 1818, d. 15 August 1876)
Director: 1876, Chairman: June – August 1876
Residences:
    Lowther Castle, Penrith; Whitehaven Castle
Landowner and colliery proprietor

C. Stanley MARTIN
Director: 1908 – 1909
Residence:
    Stainburn, Workington

William McCOWAN
    (b. c.1838. d. 7 March 1900)
Director: 1891 – 1900
Residence:
    Roseneath, Whitehaven
Other directorships:
    Distington Hematite Iron Co. (Chairman)
    Moss Bay Hematite Iron & Steel Co.
    Lowca Engineering Co.
    Whitehaven Hematite Iron & Steel Co.
    Vivian Diamond Boring Co.
    Elliscales Mining Co.
    Pallaflat Mining Co.
    Moresby Coal Co.

Albert Orlando PEECH
Director: 1920 – 1923
Residence:
    Firbeck Hall, Rotherham, Yorkshire
Other directorships:
    Steel, Peech & Tozer Ltd.
    United Steel Cos.

Sir James RAMSDEN
    (b. 23 February 1822, d. 19 November 1896)
    Knighted 1872
Director: 1878 – 1879 (resigned)
Residence:
    Abbots Wood, Barrow-in-Furness
Secretary & General Manager: Furness Railway Company
Other directorships:
    Barrow Haematite Steel Co. (Managing Director)
    Barrow Shipbuilding Co. (Managing Director)
    Barrow Flax & Jute Co.
    Barrow Steam Cornmill
High Sheriff of Lancashire
First Mayor of Barrow-in-Furness (1867 – 1872)

Sir John Scurrah RANDLES J.P., M.P.
    (b. 25 December 1857, d. 1945)
    Knighted 1905
Director: 1909 – 1923

Residence:
    Bristowe Hill, Keswick
Other directorships:
    Furness Railway Co. (1911 – 1923)
    Cockermouth, Keswick & Penrith Railway Co.
       (1910 – 1923)
    Moss Bay Hematite Iron & Steel Co.
    Workington Iron & Steel Co. (Chairman)
    Star Assurance Co.
M.P. (Conservative)
    for Cockermouth (1900 – 1906, 1906 – 1910)
    for Manchester North West (1912 – 1918)
    for Manchester Exchange (1918 – 1922)
Member of Cumberland County Council

Robert Alleyne ROBINSON
(b. 24 October 1839, d.24 November 1892)
Director: 1876 –1892,
    Deputy Chairman: 1880 – 1892
Residence:
    South Lodge, Cockermouth
Proprietor: Hampton & Facer Special Ingot Co.;
    Ellen Rolling Mills, Maryport
Chief Agent for Whitehaven Castle Estates
Other directorships:
    Solway Junction Railway Co.
    Rowrah & Kelton Fell Railway Co.
    William Baird & Co. (ironmasters)

Henry STEEL
(b.??, d. 7 October 1920)
Director: 1918 – 1920
Residence:
    Skellow Grange, Doncaster, Yorkshire
Other directorships:
    Steel, Peech & Tozer Ltd.
    United Steel Cos.

William Barrow TURNER
(b. 29 August 1840, d. 23 October 1916)
Director: 1889 – 1916
Residence:
    Ponsonby Hall, Gosforth, Whitehaven
Other directorships:
    Furness Railway Co. (1894 – 1916)
    Southern Brasilian Rio Grande do Sul Ltd.

Charles James VALENTINE
(b. September 1837, d. 5 November 1900)
Director: 1876 – 1887
Residence:
    Bankfield, Workington
Other directorships:
    Moss Bay Hematite Iron & Steel Co.
    (Joint Managing Director)
M.P. (Conservative) for Cockermouth 1885 – 1886

Sir Alexander WILSON Bt., J.P.
(b. 28 June 1836, d.??) Created Baronet ??
Director: 1887 – 1891
Residence:
    Archer House, Sheffield
Other directorships:
    Maryport & Carlisle Railway Co. (1897 – 1907)
    Charles Cammell & Co.
    (Chairman and Managing Director)
Master Cutler of Sheffield

Herbert Edward WILSON B.A. (Oxon), J.P.
(married Aline, daughter of Charles Cammell)
Director: 1916 – 1918
Residence:
    Stainburn, Workington
Other directorship:
    Maryport & Carlisle Railway Co. (1916 – 1923)

APPENDIX F

OFFICERS OF THE
CLEATOR & WORKINGTON JUNCTION RAILWAY

Accountants, Managers and Secretaries:

George Henry ANYON
Secretary & Accountant	May 1885 – 1886
Secretary	1887 – 25 Dec 1890 (died)

Thomas Steele DODGSON
Secretary & General Manager	1 March 1878 – 1885
Managing Director	13 March 1885 – 8 Jan 1891 (died)

James Allen HAYNES
Goods Manager	11 Dec 1896 – 1900
General Manager	1901 – 1907
Secretary & General Manager	1908 –1923

John LINTON
Accountant	to April 1882 (died)

Miles KNOWLES
Assistant Secretary	1892
Accountant	1893 – 1894
Assistant Secretary & Accountant	1895 – 1896
Secretary & Accountant	1897 – 1905

James PRIOR
Secretary & General Manager	1892 – 1896

Robert WOOD
Accountant	1908 – 1922

Edward. L. WAUGH
Secretary	August 1876 – February 1878

Engineers

Hugh MURRAY
Engineer & Locomotive Superintendent	1903 – 1923

A. H. STRONGITHARM
Joint Engineer	1882 – 1887

WADHAM, TURNER & CO. (Barrow-in-Furness)
Joint Engineers	July 1876 – 1880

John WOOD (Carlisle)
Joint Engineer	July 1876 – 1897

STATION OPENING & CLOSING DATES

All dates relate to public passenger services unless stated.

Archer Street
Opened: 2 June 1913
Closed: 31 May 1926
    (workmen's continued to 1 April 1929)

Arlecdon
Opened: 3 July 1883, daily
Closed: Dec 1883
    (last appearance in timetable)
Reopened: 5 Oct 1912 Saturdays only;
    closed: Dec 1916
Closed: 1 Jan 1927
    (on cessation of miners' trains)
Closed for goods traffic: 8th August 1938

Camerton Colliery Halt
Opened: 24 March 1887
Closed: by October 1923

Cleator Moor
Opened: 1 October 1879
    Renamed: Cleator Moor West from
    2 June 1924
Closed: 13 April 1931
Closed for goods traffic: 13 April 1931

Copperas Hill (LLR)
Opened: 2 June 1913
Closed: June 1921
    (last appearance in timetable)

Distington
Opened: 1 October 1879
Closed: 13 April 1931
Closed for goods traffic: 1 July 1963

Great Broughton
First appearance in timetable: Sept 1908,
    Saturdays only
Closed: Nov 1908
    (last appearance in timetable)
Closed for goods traffic: 1 September 1921

Harrington Church Road
Opened: November 1913
    (first appearance in timetable)
Closed: 31 May 1926
    (workmen's service continued to 1 April
    1929)

High Harrington
Opened: 1 October 1879
Closed: 13 April 1931
Closed for goods traffic: 1 July 1963

Keekle Colliers Platform
Opened: July 1910
Closed: 2 January 1911
Re-opened: June 1913
Closed: 1 October 1923

Linefoot
Opened: 1 September 1908
Closed: November 1908
    (last appearance in timetable)
Closed for goods traffic: 1 September 1921

Lowca LLR
Opened: 2 June 1913
Closed: 31 May 1926
    (workmen's continued to 1 April 1929)

Micklam LLR
Opened: 2 June 1913
Closed: 31 May 1926
    (workmen's continued to 1 April 1929)

Millgrove (private)
Opened: by 23 July 1903
Closed: by 1921 after use during WW1

Moresby Junction Halt
Opened: July 1910
    (first appearance in timetable)
Closed: 2 Jan 1911
Reopened: June 1913 (re-appeared in timetable)
Closed: 1 Oct 1923
    (miners' service continued, had ceased by June 1952)

Moresby Parks
Opened: 1 October 1879
Closed: 13 April 1931
Closed for goods traffic: 1 July 1963

Oatlands
Opened: 3 July 1883 daily, last in timetable Dec 1883
Sept 1888 Saturdays only to July 1892
Nov 1909 to Dec 1916
Back in timetable again July 1917 to Sept 1922
Closed: 1 Jan 1927 (miners' trains ceased)
Closed for goods traffic: 8 August 1938

Rosehill Platform (untimetabled)
In use from c.1912 to 1920s

Seaton
Opened: 4 January 1888
Wednesdays and Saturdays only from March 1891,
Saturdays only from Jan 1894, closed July 1897.
In timetable again February 1907 Saturdays only,
daily train by August 1914
Closed: Feb 1922 (last appearance in timetable)
Closed for goods traffic: 6 April 1962

Siddick Junction
Opened: 1 Sept 1880 for passenger exchange,
1 March 1890 as full station
Closed: 1 October 1934

Workington (Central)
Opened: 1 Oct 1879
Renamed from "Workington": 10 July 1880
Closed: 13 April 1931
Closed for goods traffic: 4 May 1964

APPENDIX H

SERVANTS OF THE
CLEATOR & WORKINGTON JUNCTION RAILWAY

The following list of staff is derived from several sources, including official records, the notes of the late Tom Haywood, and from a variety of other references. The list cannot claim to be complete but does include the names, jobs and dates of all known Cleator & Workington Junction Railway employees, except those who had only a very short period of service with the company (usually under six months). Dates are those of the references discovered – a span of dates does not necessarily define total length of service. More information may be available about some individuals on request to the Cumbrian Railways Association at 1 Oversands, The Esplanade, Grange-over-Sands LA11 7HH. Many staff moved from post to post round the C&WJR system so names may appear under more than one location. No responsibility can be accepted for any errors in copying or transcription; some names may appear in different forms and spellings. Company officers are included in Appendix F.

Archer Street
Stationmaster: J. Duncan (in post June 1922, also covered Church Road, also relief signalman)
J. Stuart, Booking Clerk (1913-4)

Arlecdon
Stationmaster: John Ray (at least 1922 to 1934, also Goods Agent)
Norman H. Sisson, shunter (1923, also worked Rowrah Junction)

Buckhill
Joseph Nicholson, signalman (1901-22, also covered Seaton); J. I. Fletcher, signalman (1892-3)

Calva Junction
John Martin, signalman (d.1913); William Reed, signalman (1889); Jacob Richardson, signalman (1919); William Stafford, signalman (1889); Irving Ward, signalman (1913); John Wynne, signalman (1913)

Cleator Moor
Stationmasters: Thomas Caldwell (appointed April 1879); John Hewitt (1880); John Nichol (appointed April 1889); Thomas Tyson (at least 1898 to 1901); John Allason (appointed 1901); John Dixon (appointed September 1903 to at least 1922, also Goods Agent)
Goods Agent: John Rae (appointed August 1880)
Miles Atkinson, porter/relief signalman (1900); J. Birkett, signalman (1922); J, Brennan, signalman (1922); John Byers, carter (1918); John Cunningham, platelayer (1883); A Dixon, clerk (1911); James Eldon, clerk (1916); Albert E. Frears, clerk (1920); Joseph Gainford, clerk (1890); R. W. McNichol, porter/relief signalman (1900); Joseph Morgan, porter (1906-10); John Mounsey, signalman (1881-97); E. W. Mullen, porter (1890-1); John S. Munro, porter (1891); Alfred Parr, porter/signalman (1892); Robert S. Robinson, Clerk (1896); Thomas Roe, porter (1899); J. Rogan, porter (1888-9); Alex Weir, clerk (1897); R. Wilson, porter (1899); John Wood, porter/signalman (1897); J. Wrangham, porter (1890)

Cloffocks Junction
Henry Wood, signalman (1884-99)

Derwent Branch and Sidings
Goods Agent: George Steele (resigned 1888); Joseph Park (in 1889)
Sam D. Currey, number taker (1900); T. H. Davidson, number taker (1889-91); J. Duncan, yardman (1909); James James, yardman (1900-4); T. McBride (1914); George McNichol, number taker (1905/9-10); R. W. McNichol, number taker (1889); Joseph Mitchell, signalman (1889); A. Morgan, yardman (1913-20); D. Murray, pointsman (1893-7); Arthur Parker, yardman (1906-8); Joseph H. Prior, clerk (1901-5); John Steele, clerk (1907); Thomas H. Steele, yardman (1904-6); Sam Taylor, yardman (1888); R. Wilson, number taker (1898); John Wood, pointsman (1897); John Wynne, yardman (1920)

Distington Joint
Stationmasters: John Holmes (in post, 1883); Dan Cowan (appointed 1883, dismissed 1887); William Steele (in post 1894); William Campbell (from at least 1901 to retirement in 1935)
Goods Agents: Arthur Preston Anyon (in post 1891); William Steele (appointed September 1891, also agent for Oatlands)
Miles Atkinson, porter/signalman (1902); John Bell, signalman (1880); William Brown, porter/clerk (c.1918), shunter (1919), porter/ signalman (1921); Abraham Dixon, clerk (1912-4, awarded MC for war service); John Dixon, porter (1891); Duncan Kirkpatrick, signalman (1902-22); Henry McDowell, goods clerk (1900); T. Mitchell, signalman (1902-28); Joseph Mitchell, porter/signalman (1897), signalman (1902-22); Thomas Moffatt, clerk (c.1918); Alex Mounsey, clerk (c.1918); Alfred Parr, signalman (1901-6); P. Postlethwaite, clerk (1887); John Rae, clerk (1906); Oliver Rennie, signalman (1921-8); John Seeds, signalman (1883); Thomas H. Steele, clerk (1897/9); Ernest Storey, clerk (1921-22); J. G. Unwin (1894-6)

Distington Rowrah Branch Junction
John Hodgson, signalman (1884); Duncan Kirkpatrick, signalman (1905-28); Alfred Parr, signalman (1901-6)

Dock Junction
William Crellin, signalman (1879-87); John Dixon, signalman (1898); W. Hobson, signalman (1911); Adam Holmes, signalman (1916); John S. Munro, relief signalman (1892); Sam Parker, signalman (1910); Norman H. Sisson, signalman (1922); Joseph Stephenson, signalman (1887); George Straughton, signalman (1887-1919); F. Strong, signalman (1879); Harold Taylor, signalman (1922); A. Thompson, signalman (1900); T. Thornthwaite, signalman (1901-28); R. R. Tinkler, signalman (1914); Irving Ward, signalman (1910); Peter Williamson, signalman (1913-4); Jacob Younghusband, signalman (1919)

Great Broughton
Stationmaster: Joseph W. Allason (appointed 1899, retired September 1921, aged 78, after 42 years service)
John Allason, signalman (1893)

Harrington Church Road   See Archer Street

Harrington Junction
Jonathan Banks, yardman (1912); James Bell, inspector (1883); P. Cavender, reliefman (1887); Sylvester Coady, traffic controller (1917-1922); R. Cockton, pointsman (1906-10); W. Corris, signalman (1913-28); John Cowen, signalman (1880), sub-inspector (1900); E. Dixon, clerk (1910); John Dixon, yardman (1900), signalman (1901); J. Dockray, signalman (1904-28), W. Douglas, assistant yardman (1888); William Grundell, traffic controller (1919-22); Robert S. Hewitt, traffic controller (1916-22); Frank Hill, yardman (1913); John Hodgson, guard (1897); John Hodgson, signalman (1888); Patrick Cavanagh, reliefman (1887); P. Mcguire, signalman (1914-28); Joseph Mitchell, yardman (1901); Henry Moore, pointsman (1902), signalman (1904-28); John S. Munro, signalman (1903); H. Murray, pointsman (1888); John Nichol, sub-inspector (1897); Thomas P. Norman, shunter (1914); Arthur Parker, yardman (1883, 1902-4); William Simpson, signalman (1879); William Taylor, pointsman (1895), yardman (1900); J. H. Temple, yardman (1900); J. Thompson, guard (1887); James Wilson, pointsman (1904); R. Wilson, yardman (1901); William Wilson, yardman (1887); John Wood, pointsman (1904/9-20)

High Harrington
Stationmasters: Thomas Little (appointed 1879); John Little (appointed 1881, retired 1913, died 3 Dec 1924); John Rae (appointed November 1913, still there in 1922, moved to Lazonby 1931)
E.Callaghan, signalman (1890); William Campbell, clerk (1887); W. A. Dobie, signalman (1919); Edward Doran, clerk (1918-22); Albert E. Greatorex, clerk (1919); Robert S. Hewitt, clerk (1905); Stanley T.

Jackson, clerk (c.1918); Jonathan Knights, clerk (1914); Jonathan Knowles, clerk (1907); Henry McDowell, goods clerk (1900/2-5); W. McKeating, signalman (1918); Isaac Moore, signalman (1883); Myers Murray (1900); Willliam Pattinson, clerk (1913); Joseph H. Prior, clerk (1898); J. H. Prior, clerk (1898); Hiram Roberts, clerk (1890-1); H. Roseby, clerk (1911-3); John Steele, clerk (1906); Thomas Henry Steele, junior clerk (1897)

Linefoot
Stationmasters: Daniel Dickinson (in post from 1887 to at least 1899)
Goods Agents; John Stewart Munro (in post 1904); William Fletcher (in post 1906)
John McDowell, number taker (1905); S. Mossop, signalman (1895); A. Thompson, signalman (1898); William Weightman, number taker (1906); John Wood, assistant yardman (1898); William Wright, assistant yardman (1898)

Lonsdale Dock
Goods Agent: Jacob Younghusband (appointed July 1889, retired May 1923)
Miles Atkinson, number taker (1900); William Crellin, yardsman (1879); Stanley Furguson, number taker (1906); A. Osbaldeston (jnr), signalman (1883-5); William Parker, number taker (1900); Thomas Roe, number taker (1898-1900); Thomas Rylance, yardman (1882); John Stephenson, number taker (1910); J. H. Voole, number taker (1900)

Lowca (Lowca Light Railway)
Stationmasters: Joseph Holmes (in post at 1923)
W. Corris, signalman (1913); Patrick Dalton, signalman (1916-28); J. R. Hill, signalman (1913-28)

Moresby Junction
Joseph Copeland, signalman (1888-1908); John Hewitt, signalman (1880); James Piercy, signalman (1913-14); Thomas Robinson, signalman (1879); William Stafford, signalman (1883); J. H. Temple, signalman (1908-12, 1915-22)

Moresby Parks
Stationmasters: J. C. Bonnett (appointed April 1879); Willliam Steele (appointed November 1879); John McLean (appointed July 1889, retired 31 October 1923)
Goods Agents: John (Mc)Nichol (appointed 1880); R. Higgins (in post 1894)
John Briggs, clerk (c.1918); James Edgar, signalman (1897-1913); Halliwell, signalman (1888); Joseph Hope, clerk (1920); R. Lightfoot, signalman (1916-28); J. McLean, signalman (1886); James Piercy, signalman (1913); Thomas Robinson, signalman (1879-81); Norman H. Sisson, signalman (1914); H. Temple, signalman (1915-28)

Moss Bay Branch and Sidings
James Conolly, number taker (1907), yardman (1913-22); Sam D. Currey, yardman (1904-6); John Hodgson, number taker (1887-8); James James, number taker (1994-93); A. E. Martin, yardman (1908-9); T. McBride, yardman (1911-4); George McNichol, number taker (1907); Jabez H. Merryman, number taker 1906-7); Hodgson Rey, guard (1882); George Steele, assistant guard (1887); Sam Taylor, guard (1887); J. H. Voole, (1907); R. Wilson, yardman (1900); John Wood, pointsman (1906); Jacob Younghusband, signalman (1883)

Oatlands
Stationmasters: Richard Higgins (recorded in 1894, also Goods Agent); William Campbell (recorded in 1898); Samuel Sydney McLennan (appointed May 1918); William Steele (1899, died 14 July 1918, Goods Agent from 1890)
Goods Agent: John Nichol (appointed 1880)
W. A. Dobie, porter/signalman (1922-8)

Rosehill Junction
William Cockton, signalman (1912-4); W. Corris, signalman (1912-22); Pat Mcguire, signalman (1914-28); Peter Williamson, signalman (1912)

Rowrah Junction
Goods Agent: John Ray (recorded in 1899)
John Hodgson, signalman (appointed 1887)

Seaton
Stationmasters: J. McLean (recorded in 1888); Thomas Hodgson (from 1889, resigned 26 September 1903); Joseph Gainford (appointed March 1910, still there in 1922, also Goods Agent)

Goods Agent: William Fletcher (recorded in 1911/3)
J. Nicholson, signalman (1901-28); Tom Renney, signalman (1907); Jacob Richardson, signalman (1922); Joseph Stephenson, signalman (1898); A. Thompson, signalman (1889); Fawcett Thompson, signalman (1907)

Siddick Junction
Stationmasters: A.S. Lowes (in 1901); Daniel Dickinson (in 1902)
Joseph Allason, yardman (1879); E. Callaghan, yardman (1891-5); Sam D. Currey, yardman (1900); John Dixon, yardman (1895); J. Duncan, yardman (1910-5); R. Higgins, yardman (1890); Arthur Parker, yardman (1901); William Wright, assistant yardman (1898-9)

Steel Brow
John Seeds, signalman (1902)

Workington Central
Traffic and General Manager's Departments
Stationmasters: William Allan (appointed 1879); Edward Parry Jones (in 1883); John Hewitt (appointed by 1894, died 27 July 1900); John (Mc)Nichol (appointed 1900); Roland Norman (no dates); Sylvester Coady (appointed 1 October 1914, came from Midland Rly, moved to Control Office at Harrington 1919; Thomas Leech (appointed 1919, in post at 31 December 1922)
Goods Agents: John (Jack) (Mc)Nichol (appointed 1900, died 18 June 1919); John Joseph Lunson (appointed July 1919, appointed Assistant Goods Agent, Workington (LMS), 1 January 1923, Goods Agent, Workington from 1926)
Joseph Allason, porter (1879); Arthur P. Anyon, clerk (1889); Jackson Armstrong, audit clerk (1922); T.Bassendale, signalman (1879); John Bell, guard (1913-23); Stan Benson, porter/clerk (1922); Stanley Benson, porter (c.1918); Tom Blackburn, cashier (1918-23); Robert Brown, signalman (1922); William Brown, porter/clerk (1922); William Campbell, general office clerk (1897); A. C. Cape, clerk (1908-9); Patrick Cavender, guard (1918-22); E. Clark, clerk (1894); Joseph W. Clayton, signalman (1914); Cyril Coates, clerk (c.1918); J. A. Collier, clerk (1890); Gordon Come, clerk (1912-13); John Cowen, traffic inspector (1921); John Crosthwaite, clerk (c.1918); John Cunningham, porter (1922); Joseph Currie, porter (1880); William Dalton, signalman (1887-92); Joseph E. Dawson, clerk (1915), audit clerk (1918), statistical clerk (1922); John Deans, clerk (c.1918); Joseph Dickinson, clerk (1887-91); Joseph Dickinson, porter (1890); William Dickinson, clerk (1922); J. Dixon, general office clerk (1911); J. Duncan, signalman (1922); Charles Edgar, porter (1918-22); Cyril Fenton, porter/clerk (1922); Miss K. Ferguson, clerk (c.1918); William Fletcher, audit clerk (1902); Sydney Gainford, clerk (1922); Joseph Gainford, general office clerk (1896), booking clerk (1898), passenger agent (1907); Richard Garnett, signalman (1912-28); William Grundill, signalman (c.1918); J. J. Hanna, clerk (c.1918); Raymond Haynes, clerk (c.1918); James A. Haynes, clerk (1888); managing clerk (1896), general manager (1901); Percy Hetherington, audit clerk (c.1918); Robert S. Hewitt, traffic inspector (1894), audit clerk (1908), relief station master (1920); John ("Pat") Hodgson, guard (1918-23); Thomas Hodgson, signalman (1884), reliefman (1904-5); Adam Holmes, signalman (1915-28); John W. Irving, ticket collector (1923); Stanley T. Jackson, forwarding clerk (1922); Patrick Kavanagh, guard (1917); William Kelly, clerk (1922); Miles Knowles, clerk (1881), audit clerk (1882), Auditor (1883), Assistant Secretary (1891), Assistant Secretary/Accountant (1896-1921); John W. Lancaster, clerk (c.1918); Maisie Lancaster, clerk (1919); Thomas Little, clerk (c.1918); T. McBride, assistant station manager (1915); J. McLean, booking clerk (1887); William McIntosh, porter (1888-90); R. W. McNichol, porter/relief signalman (1900-2); Thomas McVay, porter (1887); John Martin, signalman/yardman (1906); Mrs. Maxell, office attendant (1913-22); J. Mayfield, general manager's clerk (1907-9); Edith Mewhorter, accounts clerk (1918), audit clerk (1922); A. Middleton, porter (1906-9); A. H. Milburn, porter (1890); F. C. Gordon Moffat, clerk (1922); Alexander Mounsey, clerk (1922); John Mounsey, cashier's clerk (1922); Jessie Muir, clerk (1919); Thomas Mulholland, porter (1910), signalman (1922); Joseph Mulholland, clerk (1918-22); John S Munro, porter (1890), traffic inspector (1916); Myers Murray, general manager's clerk (1902-7); John Murray, porter (1885-90); David Nelson, general managers' clerk (1906), inspectors' clerk (1907-15); Dorothy Nelson, audit clerk (c.1918); John Norman, permanent way inspector (1922); Roland Norman, chief rates clerk (1922); Bessie Norman, clerk (1919); Alfred Osbaldeston, outside inspector (1879-87); Joseph Park, sub-inspector (1900), chief inspector (1906); Sam Parker, signalman (1884-1907); Willliam Parker, porter/signalman (1904-5); Joseph H. Prior, clerk (1896), booking clerk (1899); Richard Quinn, junior clerk (1919); Miss A. C. Rae, demurrage clerk (c.1918); Hodgson Reay, guard (1923); William

Reed, guard/relief signalman (1906); A. E. Renkin, porter (1888-9); John W. Richards, porter (c,1918); William Ridley (jnr), porter (1884-8); Douglas Ritson, rates clerk (1915); John Richards, porter (1922); Thomas Roe (jnr), guard (1902-22); Joseph Rogerson, guard (1890-1922); H.Roseby, clerk (1909); George Thompson, assistant accountant (1899); J.W.Todhunter, storekeeper (1892); Thomas Tyson, clerk (1901-7); B. Unwin, clerk (1885-1900); J.H.Voole, general manager's office (1900); Ada Walker, clerk (1917), audit clerk (1922); Henry Wilson, porter (1893), signalman (1900-22); William Wilson, signalman (1889), porter (1900-3); R.Wood, signalman (1899); Robert Wood, clerk (1889), head audit clerk (1899), accountant (1907-23)

Wagon Shop
Joseph Baxter, joiner (c.1918); John Brown, joiner (c.1918); Joseph W. Dawson, joiner (1906), foreman joiner (c.1911-22); Joseph Dickinson (1890); John Fisher, joiner (c.1889-1922); David Linton, joiner, (c,1918); Plaskett, joiner (1922); John R. Reid, joiner (c.1918)

Locomotive Department
A. Anderson, fireman (1890); James Anyon, locomotive foreman (1907); J. Banks, fireman (1890); Alex Beebe, driver (1922); Abe Beebe, fireman (c.1918); Henry A. Braithwaite, foreman fitter (1907), locomotive foreman (1918); Fred Braithwaite, fitter (1918-22); Walter Brown, cleaner (1918), fireman (1918), driver (1922); Joseph (Josh) Dawson, fireman (c.1918), engineman (1922); Joseph Fenton, fireman (1918), engineman (1922); John Fisher, fireman (c.1918); John Hales, loco coal man (c.1918), engineman (1922); John Howe, fireman (1908), driver (1918-22); R. Howe, fireman (1881), driver (1904); Thomas Lewin, driver (1918-22); Thomas Lumsden, fireman (1918), driver (1922); Stanley Murphy, fireman (c.1918), engineman (1922); John Murphy, striker (1918), fitter (1922); Charles Nicholson, driver (1890-1922); J. Parker, driver (1890); Bill Percy, blacksmith (c.1918); Joseph Poole, driver (1890-1922); B. Postlethwaite, fireman (1890); Andrew F. Reay, driver (1907-22); William Woodman, driver (1918-22)

Goods Department (some staff may be included in Traffic Department. above)
Alice Appleyard, clerk (c.1918); Jackson Armstrong, clerk, (1914-c.18); John Birkett, yardman (c.1918); William Brisco, yardman (c.1918); William Campbell, clerk (1890); Joseph W. Clayton, porter (1915); William Crellin, yardman (1900); Sam D. Currey, yardman (1901); Daniel Dickinson, warehouseman (1906-13); William Dickinson, clerk (1913-6); W. G. Dockray, clerk (1905-11); William Fletcher, clerk (1890); Joseph Gainford, clerk (1899); Ada Gedling, clerk (c.1918); Raymond Haynes, clerk (c.1918); Robert S. Hewitt, clerk (1900/06); Thomas R. Haywood, clerk (1917-23); Stanley T. Jackson, clerk (1916-22); William Kelly, clerk (c.1918); John Kirkbride, clerk (c.1918); John J. Knowles, clerk (1922); Joseph Lancaster, yard foreman (c.1918); William T. Lowis, cashier (1922); J. Mayfield, clerk (1909); Henry McDowell, goods manager's clerk (1899); William McKeating, yardman (c.1918); Sydney McNichol, porter (1901-2);

N. D. Melton, clerk (1909-13); Alexander Mounsey, clerk (1913-22); Jessie Muir, clerk (c.1918); John S. Munro (1901); Myers Murray, clerk (1900); Bessie Norman, clerk (c.1918); Arthur Parker, porter (1906); Alfred Parr, yardman (1890); William Pattinson, clerk (1921); Robert S. Robinson, clerk (1896-1901); Thomas Roe (jnr), porter (1890-1901); John Stephenson, porter (1907); Henry Swinburn, clerk (c,1918); Herbert Swinburn, clerk (1922); J. Tindall, clerk (1901-6); R. A. Usher, yardman (1887-1902); Irving Ward, signalman/yardman (1906); John Watson, yard foreman (c.1918); W. Waugh, clerk (1913); Henry Wood, porter (n.d.); John Wood, yardman (c.1918)

Engineer's Department
John Armstrong, fenceman (c.1918); William Beattie, foreman signal fitter (c.1918); Joseph Benson, mason (c.1918); Cyril Coates, engineer's chief clerk (1921); William Edgar, foreman mason (c.1918); Robert Edgar, mason (1923); James H. Fitzsimmons, foreman painter (1918); Isaac Fletcher, permanent way inspectors' clerk (c.1918); Sydney Gainford, engineers' clerk (1920); Harold Gilmour, painter (c.1918); Matthew Hardy, painter (c.1918); Cyril Haynes, linesman (c.1918); Charles Hewitt, linesman (c.1918); Ernest Lowther, painter (c.1918); Malcolm McKay, signal fitter (c.1918); Thomas Mitchell, fenceman (c.1918); Thomas Peel, permanent way joiner (1922); Andrew Penrice, painter (1918); William Reed, signal inspector (1908-22); William Reed, signal inspector (1911); John R. Reid, permanent way joiner (1913-22); William Tweddle, mason (1918); T. Smith, ganger/platelayer (1883-1922)

Place of work not known
Engineer's Department
Joe Bedford, platelayer (c.1918); T. Bell, permanent way rough gang (c.1918); James Boal, platelayer (c.1918); Robert Dent, sub-ganger (1903-22); Frederick Dodd, sub-ganger (1914); John Fletcher, permanent way (1920); Thomas McLure, ganger (1910-22); William McTear, platelayer (c.1918); Henry Nicholson, sub-ganger (1914-22); Albert Oliver, permanent way rough gang (c.1918); Ernest Oliver, permanent way rough gang (c.1918); William Pearson, sub-ganger (1889-1922); James Plaskett, platelayer (c.1918); Willliam Reed, platelayer (1887); William Taylor, platelayer (1885); Ernest Tubman, permanent way rough gang (c.1918); John Tweddle, mason's labourer (1897-1920); H. Wilson, platelayer (1914); John Wrenn, platelayer/sub-fenceman (1913-22)

Other staff
William Beck, passenger guard (1879); Joseph Bennett, signalman (c.1918); Matthew Brown, clerk (c.1918); Robert Brown, signalman (c.1918); Isaac Cook, signalman (1879); William Gilmour, signalman (c.1918); W. Hawke, clerk (1882); James Hill, foreman platelayer (1918-22); Robert Huck, signalman (c.1918); Mabel Little, clerk (c.1918); Patrick McQuire, signalman (c.1918); Richard Poultney, shunter/number taker (1917-22); Andy Stevens, signalman (c.1918); L. Ward, relief signalman (c.1918); Lenord Wilkinson, yardman (c.1918); John Wynne, signalman (c.1918)

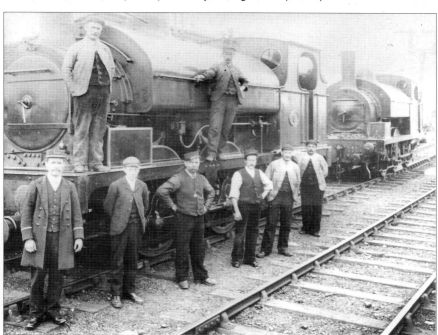

A view of staff at Distington, mainly engine crews. The locos are, first, C&WJR 0-6-0ST No. 5 "Moresby Hall", and Furness Railway 0-6-0ST No. 111. No. 111 had been rebuilt from the former Whitehaven, Cleator & Egremont Railway, No. 15 "Buttermere".

CRA Pattinson Collection PA1183

APPENDIX I

BIBLIOGRAPHY and ACKNOWLEDGEMENTS

W. McGowan Gradon appears to have used the files of *The Whitehaven News* as his principal source for writing *The Track of the Ironmasters,* especially referring to the reports of half-yearly shareholders meetings of the Cleator & Workington Junction Railway Company. The proceedings of these meetings were invariably reported verbatim in that period. To these files he would have privileged access as a director of the company of which his cousin, James McGowan, was chairman. Gradon's mother, Mrs M. A. Gradon, had also served on the board of The Whitehaven News Ltd., for sixteen years up to her death in 1948, she in turn having succeeded her father, William McGowan. Fellow directors of William McGowan at the start of the 20th century included David Ainsworth M.P. and Robert Jefferson, both directors of the C&WJR at that time (see Appendix E). William Burnyeat, another C&WJR director, had also been one of the founding directors of The Whitehaven News Ltd. in 1881, sitting alongside Robert Jefferson and William McGowan, the latter serving a total of 49 years on the board until his death in 1930. The McGowan family was to continue their close association with the newspaper until it was acquired by Cumberland Newspapers Ltd. in 1962.

The following sources were referred to in preparing the supplementary material for this book.

British Locomotive Catalogue, 1825-1923: Volume 4, *by Bertram Baxter, published by Moorland Publishing, Ashbourne, 1984.*

British Mining History No. 36: The Kelton & Knockmurton Iron Mines 1852-1923, *by R. E. Hewer, published by The Northern Mine Research Society, Sheffield, 1988.*

Centenary of the Whitehaven News 1852-1952, *published by The Whitehaven News, 1952.*

Cleator & Workington Junction Railway: History of the Railway, *compiled for the Directors, by the General Manager, January 1901. Copy of extract in Collection of Peter Robinson.*

Clinker's Register of Closed Passenger Stations and Goods Depots in England, Scotland, and Wales 1830-1977, *by C. R. Clinker, published by Avon-Anglia Publications & Services, 1978.*

Cumberland Families and Heraldry, *by C. Roy Huddlestone and R. S. Boumphrey, published by the Cumberland & Westmorland Antiquarian & Archaeological Society, 1978.*

The Cumberland Mineral Statistics 1845-1913, *by Roger Burt, Peter White and Ray Burnley, published by the Department of Economic History, University of Exeter, 1982.*

Cumbrian Railways, Journal of the Cumbrian Railways Association.

The Directory of Railway Stations, *by R. V. J. Butt, published by Patrick Stephens Ltd., 1995.*

Future of Railways, *Confidential Report produced by the General Manager for the directors of the Cleator & Workington Junction Railway, July 1921. Copy of extract in the collection of Peter Robinson.*

History, Topography and Directory of West Cumberland, *published by T. Bulmer & Co., 1883.*

The Iron & Steel Industry of West Cumberland: An historical survey, *by J. Y. Lancaster and D.R. Wattleworth, published by the British Steel Corporation, Workington, 1977.*

Railway Passenger Stations in England, Scotland and Wales: A Chronology, *by M. E. Quick, published by the Railway & Canal Historical Society, 2002.*

A Regional History of the Railways of Great Britain: Volume 14 The Lake Counties, *by David Joy, published by David & Charles, Newton Abbot, 1986.*

West Cumberland Coal 1600-1982/3, *by Oliver Wood, published by the Cumberland & Westmorland Antiquarian and Archaeological Society, 1988.*

Whitehaven: An Illustrated History, *by Daniel Hay, published by Michael Moon, Whitehaven, 1979.*

Dictionary of 20th Century British Business Leaders, *by Dr. David Jeremy and Dr. Geoffrey Tweedale, published by Bowker-Saur, 1994.*

Also: Who's Who 1923; Who Was Who 1897-1910.

Acknowledgement and thanks are due to the following persons: Michael and Peter Moon for making available to the Cumbrian Railways Association their rights to reproduce the text of the original version of *"The Track of the Ironmasters";* Peter Holmes for providing updated information on industrial locomotives; Russell Wear for updating information on the company's own locomotives; Dr. Michael Andrews for comments and additions to the supplementary notes; members of the Scottish Railway Preservation Society for information about the Scottish directors of the R&KFR; Michael Peascod for his continual support and encouragement, and for his files of detailed information on the directors of the C&WJR: members of the Cumbrian Railways email group who have patiently sought out answers to many of my questions: Alan Johnstone for producing the excellent diagrams from my sketches, and Rock Battye for his painstaking proof-reading to ensure consistency in presentation.

Photographs have been sourced from the collections of the Cumbrian Railways Association, Michael Andrews, Colour-Rail, Cumbria County Library, Michael Moon, Rae Montgomery, Ken Norman, F.W. Shuttleworth and Peter Robinson: all are individually credited as appropriate. Details of the photographic collections of the Cumbrian Railways Association may be obtained from the Photographic Services Officer, John Broughton at Bay View, Cat Tree Road, Grange-over-Sands, Cumbria LA11 7EB, enclosing a stamped addressed envelope